THE
VOICE

DR. SHARON R. RATHBUN

TATE PUBLISHING, LLC

Published in the United States of America
By TATE PUBLISHING,LLC
All rights reserved.
Do not duplicate without permission.

All Scripture references are King James Version,
unless otherwise indicated.

Book Design by TATE PUBLISHING, LLC.

Printed in the United States of America by
TATE PUBLISHING, LLC
1716 West State Highway 152
Mustang, OK 73064
(888) 361-9473

Publisher's Cataloging in Publication

Rathbun, Sharon R.

Unlocking the Mysteries of The Voice/Sharon R. Rathbun
Originally published in Mustang,OK:TATE PUBLISHING:2003
1. Spiritual 2. Religion
ISBN 0-9748244-5-3 $17.95

Copyright 2004

First Printing: April 2004

- Dedication -

To my God-fearing mother, Eunice M. Fant, who was the first to teach me of Jesus and take me to Sunday school to be taught by loving and godly teachers at a young age.

To my devoted husband, John A. Rathbun and my loving daughters, Angela R. Pollock, and Roberta J. Sharp, who have believed in me and stood by me in all my endeavors for the Kingdom of God.

To my dear friends, Ruby Skaggs and Sandra Trinidad, for all their support and encouragement for me in writing and publishing this book.

Table of Contents

Foreword 7
Preface 9
Chapter 1   Can You Hear Me Now? 11
Chapter 2   He Speaks To Us In His Word 17
Chapter 3   He Has The Voice Of An Angel . . . 31
Chapter 4   Hearing God's Voice
             In Our Visions 49
Chapter 5   He Speaks To Us In Dreams 69
Chapter 6   Discerning The Spirit
             Speaking To Us 81
Chapter 7   Hearing God's Voice in a
             Prophetic Word, or a
             Word of Knowledge 111
Chapter 8   God Speaks To Us In Song—
             He Has Perfect Pitch 123
Chapter 9   The Early Church Established
             By Heeding God's Voice 131
Chapter 10   His Voice Through Miracles 139
Chapter 11   The Heavenly Ventriloquist—
             God Speaking To Us Through
             Another As a Word of Wisdom . . 149

Chapter 12   Hearing God's Voice Of Peace . . . 159
Chapter 13   A Critical Choice—
             To Ignore or Heed The Voice 163
Bibliography 173
Endnotes 149

Foreword

Sharon Rathbun is a true servant of God. Her desire is that the believer has a pure and holy relationship with the Lord. She has a close walk with her Lord and Savior. Like the prophet Enoch, who was taken up into the throne room of God, Sharon has been called into His presence on occasion with a command from God to pray for and to work for a glorious church without spot or wrinkle. That calling has been at great risk and at great sacrifice for her, the flesh is at enmity against God and hates such a relationship, so it is no surprise that she and her husband have been met with intense opposition at every step of the way. But that is a cross that she willingly has taken.

However, for her it is not a burden to endure but a joy to be expressed with thanksgiving. It is her high calling to minister life and truth to the hearers. She does not appeal to people who have itching ears but speaks the truth in love as God's grace unfolds into changed lives. To lead others to the throne of grace is her driving ambition. And that is what this book is all about. As you read it be prepared for a

Unlocking The Mysteries Of The Voice

major shift in your commitment to Christ. You will never be the same. Sharon and her husband John are the founders and directors of Hebron Life Bible College near Blanchard, Oklahoma. That ministry focuses on both the academic and spiritual training to send forth laborers into the last days harvest. To carry out that ministry, God has equipped them for the impartation of spiritual gifts and anointings.

Dr. Richard A. Lunsford
Professor of Bible and Prophecy
American Christian College and Seminary
Oklahoma City, Oklahoma

Preface

I've had the privilege of hearing and knowing the voice of my Master since I was a very small child. And since I was so very young when the Lord began to make Himself and His voice known to me, there was no one to challenge me, that the voice I was hearing wasn't genuine and real. Hearing the Lord's voice actually started in Sunday School with all of the stories of the Bible. I would listen so intently to the Sunday School teacher as she taught the stories of the Bible, as a matter of fact. She would teach how the Lord had a voice and spoke to His children everyday. Being impressionable as a child, I believed every word that she spoke. I believed everyone could hear the voice of the Lord as Samuel, Moses, and Elijah did.

It was that very belief, which would indeed be the tool that Lord would use to shape my life for Him. From the time I was five years old and had accepted Jesus as my Savior and received His Holy Spirit, I began to hear His voice. By the time I was eight or nine years of age I had already experienced His voice of conviction.

Then, during a revival in our home church when I was sixteen years old I responded to the call of the ministry. I didn't take the call lightly as I ran down the aisle to commit myself to the mission field for the Lord Jesus Christ. At the time it didn't matter to me, where my field of labor was to be, whether in Asia, Africa, or America. I just knew I had received a commission to be about my Father's business. And still today after ministering in over fifty countries, His voice and His call still reigns in my heart and my life.

I pray that the reading of this book will enable the reader to hear with more clarity the sweetest voice one will ever hear. It is only in hearing His voice that one can truly walk in total obedience.

- Sharon R. Rathbun

Chapter 1
Can You Hear Me Now?

"Knowing His Voice is not only beneficial for the born again believer, but is absolutely necessary."

(Exodus 19:16), "And it came to pass on the third day in the morning, that there were thunders and lightning's, and a thick cloud upon the mount, and the voice of the trumpet exceeding loud; so that all the people that was in the camp trembled." (2 Samuel 22:14), "The LORD thundered from heaven, and the most High uttered his voice." (Psalm 18:13), "The LORD also thundered in the heavens, and the Highest gave his voice." (John 12:28-29), "Then came there a voice from heaven, saying, I have both glorified it, and will glorify it again. The people therefore, that stood by, and heard it, said that it thundered:"

God is still talking today, but not always in the same demonstrative way as when he spoke to the Israelites on Mount Sinai. In Isaiah God tells His people, that He was not going to speak from a mountaintop any more, where the people of God could put their hands over their ears. But instead He was going to get *inside* of the believer, by the Holy Spirit and they would have to hear Him. (Isaiah 28:10-11), "For precept must be upon precept, precept upon precept; line upon line, line upon line; here a little, and there a little: For with stammering lips and another tongue will he speak to this people." Therefore since He would be on the inside of the believer according to, (Revelation 3:20), "Behold, I stand at the door, and knock: if any man hear my voice, and open the door, I will come in to him, and will sup with him, and he with me," then His voice would always be with the child of God, as He has promised to the believer; (Hebrews 13:5), "For he hath said, I will never leave thee, nor forsake thee."

God is trying to reach His Church today, somewhat like the cellular phone commercial, that we have seen on television. "Can you hear me, now?" God is using every available tool in trying to reach us. He's not hiding from us; He is reaching out to His people. Just like the commercial, He is moving all over in our lives trying to get a response from us. Like clock-work, He is coming to our garden everyday, just as He did with Adam and Eve. It is His desire to have personal fellowship with His own, but His people are not hearing Him. It is not just for the added benefit, that the believer needs to hear Him, but it is absolutely necessary if one is to be able to respond in obedience. As it is written in, (John 10:27), "My sheep hear my voice, and I know them and they follow me:" One of the most significant reasons for hearing the Lord's voice, is so that the child of God can truly follow the Lord, wholeheartedly.

The Bible promises, that the true servant of the Lord will not follow a stranger. This can only happen as we draw near unto Him, and He will, in return, draw near to us. And as we walk with the Lord, we will begin to know Him, as our closest and dearest friend. Then, as with a very close friend, we will begin to consider what He thinks of us and what He would have us to do in every situation. You will find yourself communing with Him on an everyday basis and about everything, as one would with the dearest of friends. Thus you will fall in love with the Savior, the lover of your soul. Then, serving Him will not be a struggle, but rather a pure joy.

Though I had accepted Jesus as my Savior

and received the Holy Spirit at the age of five, it would not be until I was sixteen years old that I would truly surrender my life and destiny to Him. I began my journey with the Lord with hours of diligent study of His Word; in search of what I perceived was the absolute truth. For all of my young life I had heard so many conflicting methods of what salvation really was, and what salvation demanded from its believers. With that in mind, I decided I would search for myself extensively what true salvation entailed. That was my way of trying to secure my final destiny. I became very diligent in my Bible studies, right from the start of my conversion.

    Before each session I would have prayer, asking the Holy Spirit to reveal to me what the written Word was actually saying. I didn't want to be misled by what other people had taught me, or what their denominational beliefs were. Therefore, in my desperation to know the truth, I would begin a search that would take me on a journey of studying up to eight hours a day for many years. This was my mission in life at sixteen years of age. It was during those early years of studying His Word, that I would find myself weeping, as He was being revealed to me. He, as in the form of His Word, became so real to me that I would just pick up the Holy Bible and kiss it. For at that time it was as close as I knew in how to touch Him.

Once while I was waiting outside the grocery store for my Mother I was seated in the car, when I heard the voice of the Lord for the first time in that way. He asked me, if I knew for sure that I would live to be an old woman, would I serve Him now? One must remember I originally rededicated my life only to escape hell, particularly since seeing some of my young friends dying untimely deaths without the Lord. But, while I was in search of the real truth, something had happened to me. Without me realizing it, I had fallen in love with my Lord and Savior. While looking for the secure escape route from hell, I had come to know my Lord up close and very intimately. He was no longer just a snapshot of a picture in my mind, but rather an oil painting, a portrait engraved on my heart, as well as in my mind. For as it is written in, (Psalm 40:7), "Then said I, Lo, I come: in the volume of the book it is written of me." When one really gets to know His Lord, he will also love Him. In the car that day, I answered Him with, "I will serve you forever, because I love you with my whole being." I no longer cared how long I lived, for my destiny had been set. The Lord had become my whole life, while I was reading between the pages of the Holy Bible, and caught a glimpse of who Jesus really was. And today He still is so marvelous and lovely to this writer.

Chapter 2
He Speaks To Us In His Word

"The Bible is the most accurate way to hear from God."

King David gave many reasons for hearing the Lord's voice. In (Psalm 119:11), "Thy word have I hid in mine heart, that I might not sin against thee." (Geneva Bible Notes), "If God's word is carved in our hearts, we will be more able to resist the assaults of Satan: and therefore the prophet desires God to instruct him daily more and more in it"[1]

Even though one is saved and justified by His grace alone, the corruption of the unregenerate man still remains in the individual's flesh. Thus the work of sanctification or regeneration of the person must be accomplished by the Word of God being applied to ones life, everyday. For it is when the Word of God is allowed to be applied to the child of God, that little by little, the justified soul will come into that perfect man that Paul describes in, (Ephesians 4:13-15), "Till we all come in the unity of the faith, and of the knowledge of the Son of God, unto a perfect man, unto the measure of the stature of the fullness of Christ:" For when a man gains the knowledge of "thus saith the Word of God," in his life, he then possesses the power to control his thoughts and actions. For it is through the Word of God one will begin to put away the foolishness of the childish things of the flesh.

The Lord Jesus Himself confirmed King David's statement in, (John 15:3), "Now ye are clean through the word which I have spoken unto you." Jesus was telling His disciple that by His Word He was speaking and teaching them. He was pruning them in order for them to be a fruitful bough, where their branches would run over the wall.

Mankind is saved by confession and faith in Jesus Christ, yet it is the Word being applied to ones life that will truly change his character, for the Kingdom of God. The only way a man can be changed in his character is by the renewing of his mind, through the Word of God. It is only through His Word that one changes from glory to glory. As one is being changed inwardly as the Word is being written on his heart, he will begin to manifest that change outwardly. As the reader begins to view himself in the mirror of the written Word, the pride, the vanity, and the riotous living will began to diminish in the believer's life. Thus it is very important, for the child of God to hear the voice of God and not to harden their hearts to the written Word - that is the written Word that has been applied to one's heart by the hearing and the reading of the Word.

Hearing the voice of God not only will bring a change to a man's character, but will make him strong in the character of the Lord. (Psalm 119:28), "My soul melteth for heaviness: strengthen thou me according unto thy word." David was asking for the strength of the Word to fight not only against the temptations of sin, but also the despondency of the soul. It is through the Word of God, one can win the battle over the emotional realm of jealousy, self-pity, discouragement, grief and anger. Then Daniel confirmed it again in, (Daniel 10:19), "And said, O man greatly beloved, fear not: peace be unto thee, be strong, yea, be strong. And when he had spoken unto me, I was strengthened, and said, let my lord speak; for thou hast strengthened me."

Then in the New Testament, Apostle Paul

states that the Spirit of God, will strengthen the inner man in, (Ephesians. 3:16), "That he would grant you, according to the riches of his glory, to be strengthened with might by his Spirit in the inner man;"

(Adam Clark Commentary) states, "When one might have many enemies, cunning and strong; many trials, too great for your natural strength; many temptations, which no human power is able successfully to resist; many duties to perform, which cannot be accomplished by the strength of man; therefore you need Divine strength; ye must have might; and ye must be strengthened every where, and every way fortified by that might; mightily and most effectually strengthened. This fountain of spiritual energy can alone supply the spiritual strength which is necessary for this spiritual work and conflict."[2]

Jesus said, "The words I speak unto you are spirit and life." All these scriptures are declaring that hearing God's voice will strengthen the inner man, as well as the natural man. Then the hearing of God's voice will remove the weaknesses, fears and timidity from a child of God, as it is allowed to be written upon the tables, of ones heart. Through the Word of God, the born again believer can declare, as Apostle Paul did in (Philippians 4:13), "I can do all things through Christ which strengthened me." For Paul had learned through his experiences, that there was nothing in this world that he could not do, if the Lord allowed it to transpire in his life.

In the following scripture, it says that hearing the voice of God, in His Word, will quicken the hurting child of God, if he can hear and recognize His voice. (Psalm 119:107), "I am afflicted very much: quicken me, O LORD, according unto thy word." Being quickened actually means, that through the Word of God a person can be repaired, restored, recovered, and to be made alive and whole. Then, one can see by these scriptures just how important it is to know and hear the precious voice of God in today's society.

Knowing His voice is not only beneficial for the born again believer, but is absolutely necessary. For it is only by knowing and hearing the voice of God, that we can truly know the right instructions and the Godly wisdom, that one needs in this life. Hence, hearing and knowing His Word is the key, for being able to live our lives as an instrument of God. All the benefits and equipment one will ever need to accomplish God's will can always come through the knowing and the hearing of the voice of God in His written Word.

Most of the real Church today would agree with the importance of hearing the voice of the Lord. And yet you will find that not many of the saints actually *hear* His voice, even occasionally? Many of the Christians today, because of their busy lives, are not even desiring or searching for His true voice. Yet, in this generation the child of God needs to hear His voice, more than any other generation before. In this day the Church must rise to the occasion; to not only hear His voice but also *be* His voice of life and power to minister to a lost, dying and confused world.

You would think, with all the questions and confusions that the saints are facing in every corridor of their life, that they, like King David, would cry out, (Psalm 42:1-2), "As the hart panteth after the water brooks, so panteth my soul after thee, O God. My soul thirsteth for God, for the living God: when shall I come and appear before God?"

The people of God must seek the *face* of God and not just the *hand* of God that they might be spared so many of the heartaches they are encountering today. God's Word promises that if the people of

God hear His voice they would not be caught up in so many traps of the world – traps meant to choke out the things of the Lord. (Psalm 81:8-14), "Hear, O my people, and I will testify unto thee: O Israel, if thou wilt hearken unto me; there shall no strange god be in thee; neither shalt thou worship any strange god. I am the LORD thy God, which brought thee out of the land of Egypt: open thy mouth wide, and I will fill it. But my people would not hearken to my voice; and Israel would none of me. So I gave them up unto their own hearts' lust: and they walked in their own counsels. Oh that my people had hearkened unto me, and Israel had walked in my ways! I should soon have subdued their enemies, and turned my hand against their adversaries." As one reads these verses today, it is very apparent that God was pleading with Israel, as He is with the Church today, to listen to His voice. He is saying, "listen to my voice, then you will not be deceived into going astray by picking up the false satisfactions and desires, that only tend to be false gods in your life." But, Israel instead, walked, in their counsel and thus rejected God's counsel of His Word.

    When one listens to His voice, He always puts the right answer in their mouth. The answer He puts in ones mouth will be right every time, because the answer will be the Word written on one's heart. It is when God's children obey the instruction of the Lord's voice that the enemy will stay under their feet where he belongs.

Of course there are always going to be some, of His children that will learn everything the hard way, because they will not listen to the Lord's voice of instruction and wisdom. Even as the Word is being preached in their own churches, they are deciding in their hearts that it is not the Word for them. They automatically lean upon their own counsel and the lust of their own hearts. And through their own decisions, time and time again, they live a life of heartaches and destruction.

For the most part this is the very reason that many of God's children, like the nation of Israel, have needlessly suffered so much pain in their lives. Yet, our God has always desired and longed for the fellowship of His children, because He wants a love relationship. As He said in, (Isaiah. 1:18-19), "Come now, and let us reason together, saith the LORD: If ye be willing and obedient, ye shall eat the good of the land:" If the child of God will allow the Lord's voice of the Word to have preeminence in his life, he, also can have and enjoy the "good of the land."

The more evident way to hear from the Lord today is through the reading and studying of the Bible. Also it is the most accurate way to hear from God since holy men of God, through the inspiration of the Holy Spirit, wrote it. King David said in, (Psalm 119:140), "Thy Word is very pure: therefore thy servant loveth it." Then in, (Psalm 119:160), "Thy Word is true from the beginning:" David, by the inspiration of the Holy Spirit, was saying that from the foundations of the world and before time began for man, the Word, which was "with God and *was* God" was always the absolute truth. Even before His holy prophets had penned him, the Word, in ink, He was there all the time as the Word of truth, as it is written in, (John 17:17), "Thy Word is truth."

Many times in my own life when I was encountering battles far greater than I, and my own strength seemed to be edging out of me, I would "look unto the hills," from where my help has always come from. Then, I would cry unto the same God that King David cried unto, with the words, "Lead me to that rock that is higher than I." That rock being, Jesus, who is the voice of the written

Word. Then while in the presence of God, by His Holy Spirit, He would remind me of what "thus saith the Word of the Lord." And with that living Word came peace like a river unto me. And with the reminder of what His Word declares, would also come the instruction and the wisdom I needed. It was that same Word of God, which is the "lamp unto the saints feet and the light unto their path," (Psalm 119:105). (Adam Clark's Commentary), gives the example, "God's word is a candle which may be held in the hand to give us light in every dark place and chamber; and it is a general light shining upon all his works, and upon all our ways."[3]

When the child of God is in a battle and he needs desperately to hear His voice of instruction, he will hear that voice, from behind him; the voice that he has heard so many times before, because that voice has been recorded on the table of his heart, through the reading and hearing of the written Word. When one hears or reads the written Word of God and allows it to be applied to his heart, it will be there when he needs it the most. As in, (Isaiah 30:21), "And thine ears shall hear a word behind thee, saying, This is the way, walk ye in it, when ye turn to the right hand, and when ye turn to the left."

Since God is the same yesterday, today and forever, so has the Word of God been settled in heaven and cannot be changed, (Psalm 119:89), "Thy word is settled in heaven." Isaiah declares the same words in, (Isaiah 40:8), "The Word of our God shall stand forever." The strongest voice of God in the earth today, for those who have an ear to hear, is the Holy Bible. When the Bible has become the voice of God to the hearer, the Bible becomes a delight and great spoils to the soul, who embraces it. For when the child of God allows His Holy Word to speak to them in all of life's matters, he will have God's great peace upon his life.

To study and meditate upon the Word of God will cause God's people to triumph, with unshakeable confidence in their God, in every situation. Studying and applying the Holy Word to ones heart will cause one to have all the faith they will ever need, to face and conquer any obstacles that might be placed before them. To hear the voice of the written Word of God is like having weapons for every warfare at your disposal, for a mere price of acceptance.

There are even blessings that have been promised to the reader and the believer.

Unlocking The Mysteries Of The Voice

(Deuteronomy 28:1-2), "And it shall come to pass, if thou shalt hearken diligently unto the voice of the LORD thy God, to observe and to do all his commandments which I command thee this day, that the LORD thy God will set thee on high above all nations of the earth: And all these blessings shall come on thee, and overtake thee, if thou shalt hearken unto the voice of the LORD thy God." (The Jamieson-Fausset-Brown Commentary) states, "So that on the first entrance of the Israelites into the land of promise, their whole destiny was laid before them, as it was to result from their obedience or the contrary."[4] Oh, how often God's desires for us are far greater than ours, if only we would hear and obey His voice.

God told Joshua right after Moses died, for him to "be strong and very courageous, that he may observe to do according, to all the law, which Moses His servant commanded him to do." God told Joshua not to stray from what he had been taught by Moses. But if a person will read on, he will find that there was a positive way to accomplish that commandment. (Joshua 1:8), "This book of the law shall not depart out of thy mouth; but thou shalt meditate therein day and night, that thou mayest observe to do according to all that is written therein: for then thou shalt make thy way prosperous, and then thou shalt have good success." In essence, God was telling Joshua to keep the Word of the Lord, before him at all times, and then he would stay strong. The Bible then must be read and heard on a continual basis, for the child of God to be strong in what he has been persuaded in. *Read* the Word, *memorize* the Word, *believe* the Word, and then with boldness *declare* the Word!

Chapter 3
He Has the Voice of an Angel

"Everyday, angels are ministering to the people of God, as a voice of the Lord, but we remain unaware."

God may speak through the voice of an angel whom you may have believed to be only a stranger. Everyday angels are ministering to the people of God, as a voice of the Lord, but we remain unaware. Apostle Paul wrote in, (Hebrews 1:14), "Are they not all ministering spirits, sent forth to minister for them who shall be heirs of salvation?" God created the angels to minister to the born again believers. Angels were not used to minister unto mankind until the time of Abraham, who is a type of those who receive salvation by faith, being the heirs of salvation.

However, the first time one reads of an angel ministering in the Bible, it is to Hagar and not to Abraham. But, Hagar was under the covering of

Abraham, plus she was already carrying Abraham's son Ishmael. (Genesis 16:7-8),"And the angel of the LORD found her by a fountain of water in the wilderness, by the fountain in the way to Shur. "And he said, Hagar, Sarai's maid, whence camest thou and whither wilt thou go? And she said, I flee from the face of my mistress Sarai." The angel of the Lord ministered to Hagar and told her she would have a son and he would be a great nation. Later, the angel would minister to Hagar again when she thought her son was going to die; (Genesis 21:17), "And God heard the voice of the lad; and the angel of God called to Hagar out of heaven, and said unto her, what aileth thee, Hagar? Fear not; for God hath heard the voice of the lad where he is." The angel was God's voice to Hagar, assuring her that He had not forgotten her and her son's frailties or their framework. (Psalm 103:14), "He knoweth our frame; he remembereth that we are dust."

    I once had a similar experience with an angel like Hagar's encounter, when I was eighteen years old, and living hundreds of miles away from my family. It was on a very hot day in Texas, when I didn't have the luxury of an air-conditioned home. I decided to take a ride in my car since it was air conditioned so I could cool off. Now, in the early sixties the Church was more demanding on how the saints should dress and I had been raised to dress that way. But since I didn't live with my parents, anymore, I took my freedom liberally. On that particular day, I was wearing a short outfit, which had a cute skirt that matched it, so that I could put it on when going out in public. As I was walking toward the car, I heard that still small voice within me say, "You had better go back after the skirt and your purse." Well, I was in a hurry and thought within myself, "I will only be gone for a short while and no one can see me in the car anyway."

As I was enjoying the nice cool ride in my car, it began to act strange like it was running out of gas. I decided I would pull into a shopping plaza for a while and shut the car off. Sure enough, when I tried to start it again, it was dead. I knew no one I could call to help me. I thought of contacting the church where I was attending and teaching a Sunday school class. However, I didn't want the church crowd to see me dressed as I was. Suddenly I felt trapped and very naked.

As I walked to a bus stop on Berry Street in Fort Worth, Texas, it took everything within me, not to fall apart, even though I felt like it. When I got to the bus stop, I saw a gas station behind it. But, I didn't have that kind of money with me, so I waited for the bus. Oh, how I have learned to listen to the still small voice within me. I waited long enough at the bus stop, to get sunburned as well as to make God and myself, plenty of vows. I vowed to the Lord that should He just get me out of that situation, without anyone I knew seeing me, I would never again go anywhere dressed inappropriately where I would be ashamed to be seen.

When the bus pulled up at the curb, only one man and myself boarded, on an empty bus. I walked almost to the back of the bus and sat down on the left side and turned my face toward the window. I was still wondering how I would get out of this situation, when suddenly a man dressed like the bus driver, bent over to me and asked, "Why are you crying?"

I was only crying on the inside where no one could see me cry. Then for some reason I cannot explain, I told him of my problem. He said to me, "Come with me," and like a child, I followed him off the bus. He walked with me to the gas station, where he instructed the mechanic of where my car was and what it needed. As he was paying for the work to be done on my car, I over heard him say to the mechanic that if it cost any more, that he would take care of it. He claimed that he came that way all the time, so he would be by there to pay whatever the difference was. I was so embarrassed that I began to assure him; that I never take money from strangers, so I would be back there tomorrow to pay him back.

Tomorrow came and I went searching for the kind bus driver who had helped me. When the bus drove up to the curb that day and many days afterwards, it was never the same bus driver who had helped me in my distress. I finally asked the bus driver, who was driving the bus, "Where is the other bus driver who drove this bus before?" The bus driver answered, "Lady, I have driven this bus for over twenty some years and the only time, I am not driving this bus, is when I am on vacation." He proceeded to tell me his vacation would not be for a few months yet and no one else had driven his bus. I went home that day still not knowing what had taken place or whom I had encountered.

It would be another seven years, before I would know that God had sent His angel to rescue me on that hot summer day in Texas. The next time I would see that angel, would be when I experienced

Unlocking The Mysteries Of The Voice

a journey beyond this world in a vision. In fact, this same angel would appear to me five more times in five different dreams, over the next thirty-one years. Each time the angel appeared to me in a dream was always at the point of a major change in my life and ministry. Everyday angels are ministering to the people of God somewhere, as a voice of the Lord, unaware. (Hebrews 13:2), "Be not forgetful to entertain strangers: for thereby some have entertained angels unaware." There are indeed angels and they have and are used as a voice of God, to His people.

    Some of the names of God's angels are mentioned in the Bible, as well as their rank among the other angels. Gabriel and Michael are both first mentioned in the Bible starting in the book of Daniel. It is the voice of God who introduces Gabriel to Daniel when He tells Gabriel to explain the vision to Daniel in, (Daniel 8:16), "And I heard a man's voice between the banks of Ulai, which called, and said, Gabriel, make this man to understand the vision." The name of Gabriel means, "strength of God," and he is most likely over all the messenger angels, since Gabriel is the angel that is used so often to explain to the people of God, what

God had said or shown in a vision. Though angels are highly intelligent, they only tell what they are commissioned to report, by their Creator.

The first encounter with Gabriel was in a vision, but the next time Daniel sees Gabriel while he was in prayer. (Daniel 9:21), "Yea, while I was speaking in prayer, even the man Gabriel, whom I had seen in the vision at the beginning, being caused to fly swiftly, touched me about the time of the evening oblation." An angel can appear in dreams and visions with a message from God, and can even explain the meaning of the message while still in the dream or vision. But, an angel can also appear in human form to a child of God, with a message from the Lord or even to help one of God's children.

We see this in the New Testament when Gabriel shows up in the temple with Zacharias announcing that he and Elizabeth would have a son named, John. This was a very important birth since John would be the forerunner of Jesus Christ. Also when Elizabeth was in her sixth month, Gabriel appears to Mary with the announcement she would give birth to the Son of God. He also explained to her how this birth would take place even though she was a virgin. (Luke 1:26-27), "And in the sixth month the angel Gabriel was sent from God unto a city of Galilee, named Nazareth, To a virgin espoused to a man whose name was Joseph, of the house of David; and the virgin's name was Mary." (Luke 1:32-35), "And, behold, thou shalt conceive in thy womb, and bring forth a son, and shalt call his name JESUS. He shall be great, and shall be called the Son of the Highest: and the Lord God shall give unto him the throne of his father David: And he shall reign over the house of Jacob for ever; and of his kingdom there shall be no end. Then said Mary unto the angel, how shall this be, seeing I know not a man? And the angel answered and said unto her, The Holy Ghost shall come upon thee, and the power of the Highest shall overshadow thee: therefore also that holy thing which shall be born of thee shall be called the Son of God."

    All of the scriptures about the angel Gabriel, and what seems to be his commission, portrays him always as the messenger of God. He also explains 'what, how and where' concerning the messages. This could very well be revealing Gabriel's rank and position. He is most likely over all the angels that are sent to give a message, from God. Gabriel announces in, (Luke 1:19), that he stands in the presence of God, which suggests, that the position he holds is of some high order. And since it was Gabriel that announced the most important announcement of the birth of Jesus, seems to indicate again of his very high position. Then in, (1Thessalonians 4:16), "For the Lord himself shall descend from heaven with a shout, with the voice of the archangel, and with the trump of God: and the dead in Christ shall rise first." (J. Rodman Williams) states in, "The voice of the archangel, could very well mean literally an archangel voice, not with just an angel's voice. That archangel would most likely be Gabriel's voice."[1] This could mean that Gabriel would be in a rank as to have a third of the angels under his command. This statement will be explained later in this chapter.

    The Archangel Michael is first introduced by the angel Gabriel to Daniel when he tells him of the battle he had been encountering with the King of Persia and needed Michael's help, (Daniel 10:13), "But the prince of the kingdom of Persia withstood me one and twenty days: but, lo, Michael, one of the chief princes, came to help me; and I remained there with the kings of Persia." Also Gabriel tells Daniel one more time how Michael is helping him fight in,

(Daniel 10:21), "But I will show thee that which is noted in the scripture of truth: and there is none that holdeth with me in these things, but Michael your prince." Later on it is Gabriel that tells Daniel how Michael will be fighting for the Jews in the latter days in, (Daniel 12:1), "And at that time shall Michael stand up, the great prince which standeth for the children of thy people: and there shall be a time of trouble, such as never was since there was a nation even to that same time: and at that time thy people shall be delivered, every one that shall be found written in the book."

In these scriptures Michael is called by Gabriel, the Prince, the Great Prince and the Chief Prince, while Jude calls Michael, the Archangel, but he is always a fighter. The Bible explains to the reader how Michael fought with Satan twice, once for the body of Moses and to rid heaven of Satan and his fallen angels. (Jude 1:9), "Yet Michael the archangel, when contending with the devil he disputed about the body of Moses, durst not bring against him a railing accusation, but said, The Lord rebuke thee." (Revelations 12:7-9), "And there was war in heaven: Michael and his angels fought against the dragon; and the dragon fought and his angels, and prevailed not; neither was their place found any more in heaven. And the great dragon was cast out, that old serpent, called the Devil, and Satan, which deceiveth the whole world: he was cast out into the earth, and his angels were cast out with him." Michael, the archangel, is defiantly over the warring angels as John, the Revelator, states, "Michael and his angels fought against the dragon and his angels."

Another reason for the conclusion of Michael and Gabriel being over the remaining two thirds of the angels of God is because much of what God created was in the form of *three's*. Like when He created the earth with space, time and matter and grasses, herbs, and trees. Then when God created man in, (Genesis 1:25), "And God said, Let us make man in our image, after our likeness:" That is exactly what He did by making man a body, soul, and spirit to reveal Himself as a Triune God. Yet He is one God, as man is one, yet with *three* very important components. That is why it only seems to be in line with God's character in creation, that He would have three Archangels.

Also when Satan took a *third* of the angels with him when he fell, leaving two *thirds* of the angels remaining in the heavens, it seems very likely that Michael and Gabriel could have been over the other two thirds of the angels. Especially since Michael would be over the warring angels, as we always see him fighting for the plans of God and His Kingdom. While Gabriel would be most likely over the messenger angels, since most of his commission is related to giving a message to someone for God.

This leaves one to believe that Satan was over the worship and music as in, (Ezekiel 28:13), "the workmanship of thy tabrets and of thy pipes was prepared in thee in the day that thou wast created." For the word workmanship there means, deputyship, ministry or occupation, while tabrets means, a tambourine and timbrel, and pipes means, a musical wind instrument, consisting of a tube with holes, like a flute or clarin.

Angels were created by God and are mentioned as early as Genesis, and they are mentioned as an instrument of Jesus and His voice, even till the last chapter of Revelations. After man had been evicted from paradise and lost his original state, in the image of God, he could no longer see or hear spiritually, to communicate with God who is a Spirit, until the new Adam came, which would be our Lord, Jesus. Man from that time on would be ruled by his five, physical senses, instead of the Spirit of God. Then God out of His mercy began to send His angels to mankind, as an instrument of His voice, so that man could actually see with his eyes, the angels of the Lord and thus be able to hear God's voice.

God used the voice of His angels to warn Lot of the impending destruction of Sodom and Gomorrah in, (Genesis 19:12-13), "And the men said unto Lot, Hast thou here any besides? Son in law, and thy sons, and thy daughters, and whatsoever thou hast in the city, bring them out of this place: For we will destroy this place, because the cry of them is waxen great before the face of the LORD; and the LORD hath sent us to destroy it." As a voice of God, angels are many times used to warn the believers. The person being warned by an angel may think that it is only a stranger or a visitor, that has warned them. One would have to wonder if Lot even knew for sure that these men were angels, since Abraham was also called Lord, in those days out of respect. If he knew, why was he trying to protect the angels, from the wicked, perverted men, in Sodom and Gomorrah? Are they not stronger than man? Indeed they are, and death is not a part of their framework. Also, it was not until the twelfth verse that the angels warned Lot of the destruction, so it is possible that Lot did not know they were angels.

God's voice through an angel can be very rough, as in a command like we see in, (Exodus 23:20-22), "Behold, I send an Angel before thee, to keep thee in the way, and to bring thee into the place which I have prepared. Beware of him, and obey his voice, provoke him not, for he will not pardon your transgressions, for my name is in him. But if thou shalt indeed obey his voice, and do all that I speak; then I will be an enemy unto thine enemies, and an adversary unto thine adversaries."

After Elijah had killed the false prophets of Baal he became depressed, because of Jezebel's threat that she would have him killed. It was the angel of the Lord that God used to minister to him twice to revive him, (1Kings 19:7-8), "And the angel of the LORD came again the second time, and touched him, and said, Arise and eat, because the journey is too great for thee. And he arose, and did eat and drink, and went in the strength of that meat forty days and forty nights unto Horeb the mount of God."

And we see again God sending His angel to minister to Daniel in, (Daniel 6:22), "My God hath sent his angel, and hath shut the lions' mouths, that they have not hurt me: forasmuch as before him innocence was found in me; and also before thee, O king, have I done no hurt."

God can and does send His angels as His voice, not only for desperate needs, but to tell His servant what they are called to do, as He did with me. This is particularly important to a child of God who has not an inkling of the purpose for their life. God, not willing that His servant's calling be wasted, uses an angel in Gideon's life, (Judges 6:11-12), "And there came an angel of the LORD, and sat under an oak which was in Ophrah, that pertained unto Joash the Abiezrite: and his son Gideon threshed wheat by the winepress, to hide it from the Midianites. And the angel of the LORD appeared unto him, and said unto him, The LORD is with thee, thou mighty man of valour." (Judges 6:16), "And the LORD said unto him, surely I will be with thee, and thou shalt smite the Midianites as one man."

It was not known to Gideon, that he had been visited, and talked to, by an angel, until after the angel was gone. The angel had eaten and showed Gideon how to offer an offering unto the Lord and yet Gideon knew not whom he was.

Later, you'll recall it was an angel that announced the birth of Jesus, to some shepherds in a field, (Luke 2:10-11), "And the angel said unto them, Fear not: for, behold, I bring you good tidings of great joy, which shall be to all people. For unto you is born this day in the city of David a Savior, which is Christ the Lord." Then thirty-three years later it was angels, who announced the resurrection of Jesus, (Matthew 28:5-6), "And the angel answered and said unto the women, Fear not ye: for I know that ye seek Jesus, which was crucified. He is not here: for he has risen, as he said. Come, see the place where the Lord lay." *Angels are certainly the voice for the Lord.*

In (Luke 4:10), "For it is written, He shall give his angels charge over thee, to keep thee:" The word "charge" means command. God sends His angels many times to give His servants commands that will change their life. An angel gave Peter and John a command to go and preach in the temple to the people. That was a command: (Acts 5:18-20), "But the angel of the Lord by night opened the prison doors, and brought them forth, and said, Go, stand and speak in the temple to the people all the words of this life."

Another time an angel spoke as a command from God was recorded in (Acts 8:26), "And the angel of the Lord spake unto Philip, saying, Arise, and go toward the south unto the way that goeth down from Jerusalem unto Gaza, which is desert."

God has and does still speak to His children through the voice of angels. God spoke to Cornelius through the voice of an angel in, (Acts 11:13-14), "And he showed us how he had seen an angel in his house, which stood and said unto him, Send men to Joppa, and call for Simon, whose surname is Peter; Who shall tell thee words, whereby thou and all thy house shall be saved." Also the Apostle Peter had an angel come and speak to him in, (Acts 12:7-8), "And, behold, the angel of the Lord came upon him, and a light shined in the prison: and he smote Peter on the side, and raised him up, saying, Arise up quickly. And his chains fell off from his hands. And the angel said unto him, Gird thyself, and bind on thy sandals. And so he did. And he saith unto him, Cast thy garment about thee, and follow me."

Paul had an angel come and speak unto him, as a voice of the Lord in (Acts 27:23-24), "For there stood by me this night the angel of God, whose I am, and whom I serve, saying, Fear not, Paul; thou must be brought before Caesar: and, lo, God hath given thee all them that sail with thee."

One by one through out the Old and New Testaments, God had a voice through His angels. Their voice could go into locked prisons, or on the raging seas, to speak as the oracles of God to His chosen people. The next time you are talking to a stranger that has come to help you; you just might be talking to an angel, as a voice of God.

Chapter 4
Hearing God's Voice in our Visions

"Some visions have been so powerful and dramatic that even the prophets trembled with fear."

Visions are another way of God reaching and speaking to His people. A vision can take place while you are wide-awake or asleep in your bed. A vision at night, while you are asleep is called a *night* vision. It is different than a dream in the night. Night vision means you are seeing a sight or that you have been allowed to take a look at something. A vision that one has when he is awake is a sight (mental) vision. It can be a revelation or an oracle. It can also be as a view (as the act of seeing), the appearance or shape of the thing. It can be as though one is looking into a mirror or a looking glass.

In the Bible, most of the visions that were given were to God's true prophets and prophetesses that wholly followed the Lord. The first time that a vision from God is mentioned in the Bible is in, (Genesis 15:1), "After these things the word of the Lord came unto Abram in a vision, saying, Fear not, Abram: I am thy shield, and thy exceeding great reward." Genesis 15:5-6, "And he brought him forth abroad, and said, look now toward heaven, and tell the stars, if thou be able to number them: and he said unto him, so shall thy seed be. And he believed in the LORD; and he counted it to him for righteousness." God was talking directly to Abraham and showing him, what He was going to give him, through this vision. Abraham was wide-awake for this vision.

    Even though the Bible says, God had spoken to Abraham twice before, but for some reason doesn't call the encounters, visions. It may be that God just appeared unto him, we do not know. The scriptures don't tell for sure if the other two previous encounters were a vision. (Genesis 12:4), "So Abram departed, as the LORD had spoken unto him; and Lot went with him: and Abram was seventy and five years old when he departed out of Haran." (Genesis 12:7), "And the LORD appeared unto Abram, and said, unto thy seed will I give this land: and there builded he an altar unto the LORD, who appeared unto him." The word "appeared" can, also be called vision, which would mean that (Genesis 12:7), could have been another vision that Abraham had. And if that was a vision, then, (Genesis 17:1) was also a vision. For it was in (Genesis 17:1-4), that God was reinforcing His promise to Abraham again, that he would indeed have an heir. *And God was using a vision to remind Abraham that He had not changed his promise.*

Later on, Abraham's grandson, Jacob, received a vision from God, instructing him not to be afraid to go down to Egypt. Egypt is where Joseph, his beloved son, was reigning, second from the throne, but Jacob didn't even know that Joseph was alive. Therefore God had to speak to Jacob in a vision in (Genesis 46:2). Through that vision, God made three promises to Jacob. He promised Jacob that He would go with him into Egypt; and yet, not leave him there forever. He also promised to make Jacob, whose name had been changed to Israel, a great nation, (Genesis 46:2-4).

There was a time in Samuel's day, that God withheld His voice from His people. It was in a time of darkness, when there was no one receiving visions or dreams from God. When God *did* choose to speak, He chose to speak in a vision to a young boy, named Samuel. Samuel would hear and obey God's voice, thus becoming the greatest prophet of his day.

Everything that Samuel spoke as the oracles of God always came to pass, (1 Samuel 3:19), "And Samuel grew, and the LORD was with him, and did let none of his words fall to the ground." It was while Samuel was still a child; God gave the young prophet, a vision concerning his mentor, Eli, the Priest, and his house. The vision was so real and distinct, that the voice actually seemed to be Eli's voice, a human voice. In the vision God stood and talked to Samuel clearly, while Samuel was in a wide-awake state. (1 Samuel 3:10), "And the LORD came, and stood, and called as at other times, Samuel, Samuel. Then Samuel answered, speak; for thy servant heareth." When an individual has this kind of a vision, he will see it as though a man is speaking directly to him in the flesh; to the point that the one having the vision will not be able to do anything else during that vision.

Sometimes the person will wonder if he is "in or out of the body," while having this experience, as Apostle Paul did. Paul himself said he didn't know for sure. (2Corinthians, 12:2-4), "I knew a man in Christ above fourteen years ago, (whether in the body, I cannot tell; or whether out of the body, I cannot tell: God knoweth;) such an one caught up to the third heaven. And I knew such a man, (whether in the body, or out of the body, I cannot tell: God knoweth;) How that he was caught up into paradise, and heard unspeakable words, which it is not lawful for a man to utter." Later Paul recounts that same vision in, (Acts 26:19), "Whereupon, O king Agrippa, I was not disobedient unto the heavenly vision:"

    Ezekiel experienced the same kind of a vision in, (Ezekiel 8:3-4), "And he put forth the form of an hand, and took me by a lock of mine head; and the spirit lifted me up between the earth and the heaven, and brought me in the visions of God to Jerusalem, to the door of the inner gate that looketh toward the north; where was the seat of the image of jealousy, which provoketh to jealousy. And, behold, the glory of the God of Israel was there, according to the vision that I saw in the plain."

    I can actually relate to this vision, because when I was twenty-five years of age, I had a similar vision. I am not going to tell all that was shown to me in that particular vision, but I am going to share some of it. I do not know even after thirty-five years, if I was "in the body or out of the body." But I do know it was so real, that to me it actually happened and I can still see it all just as clearly today as it was then.

I was asleep in bed, when I was awakened by the sound, of what sounded like a helicopter to me. Then I heard a voice speaking, telling me not to be afraid. I then began to float upward. While floating upward, I looked down and saw my body still on the bed, yet my body that was moving upward, looked just like my body that was still on the bed. The reason that I could see so clearly down on my bed was because I was not facing toward the sky. It was as though there was a propeller right above my waist that was pushing me upward. This was not at all like I had seen in pictures of how the saints were supposed to exit during the rapture. That experience had led me to believe since that time, that where that propeller feeling and sound was could very well be where the spirit man reigns within us. (John 7:38-39), "He that believeth on me, as the scripture hath said, out of his belly shall flow rivers of living water. But this spake He of the Spirit, which they that believe on Him should receive: For the Holy Ghost was not yet given; Because Jesus was not yet glorified."

I went past what looked like to me to be planets of some kind, in a dark firmament, while I was en route to somewhere. Then I landed somewhere that looked a lot like the earth, as far as plants and buildings go. While being there I saw people from my past that I had known as a child. They were sitting on pews in a building that had a platform that looked like the inside of a church. Then while sitting in that building, a man I had seen only once before, was on the platform. He pointed his hand toward me and began to prophesy to me. When he had finished prophesying, he asked if I understood what he had prophesied. I shook my head, no. He then told me to wait until afterwards and he would explain to me the meaning of his words that he had spoken to me.

After everyone but he and I were gone, he took me to what looked like an architect's drawing board. There on the board was my entire life from the beginning to the end. As I was looking at the drawing, the man in the vision asked me where I was in my life, at that time, and to indicate that on the drawing board. I pointed to an oblong box that was connected to two lines. The line had started from the left side at the bottom of the drawing and reached to the left side of the bottom of the oblong box on the drawing. Then on the right side, at the top of the oblong box, the line began again and ended at the top of the right side of the drawing; which placed the oblong box in the middle of the two lines. When I pointed to the oblong box, to where I thought I was, according to the drawing, he agreed with me. He then proceeded to tell me I was with child and that I would have to go into the wilderness, for the sake of the child's life. As I walked away from the man toward the wilderness, I looked and felt as though I was in my ninth month and ready to be delivered.

    The next thing, that I remember was myself coming down and approaching my bed. The closer I came toward the bed, the more I thought I was getting into the wrong end of the bed. I no sooner was in the bed, when my husband was awakened and asking me "Where have you been?" He was a person who could hear the wind coming through just one single window blind, yet he never heard me leave the bed. But, he felt me as I was getting back into the bed and he told me I was at the wrong end of the bed. I believe, that in that vision the child I was carrying represented the *ministry* that was going to be birthed within me.

For within the next two short years, I would be in full time ministry. Things started happening almost immediately from that day to move me into the will of God for my life. In the vision, I would have to go to the wilderness, for the sake of the child that was within me. The reason being - I would have to leave all my loved ones for the birthing of the ministry. The ministry God had planned for me would have been smothered, very early on, if I had not been alone for the birthing. For I had, all my life, cared far too much for what my family and others thought of the decisions I made. At that time, I was still seeking for their approval in whatever God would show me, to the point the Lord told me one day, that He didn't need an interpreter to explain His words to me. He knows His children and He knows how to speak with clarity to His children.

Peter, James and John had a vision on the Mount of Transfiguration, where they saw Jesus, Moses and Elias. The vision was so real, that Peter began to tell Jesus that there should be three tabernacles built for all three of the men, in the vision. One of the amazing things is that all three of the Apostles had the same vision, at the same time. And it was indeed a vision as stated by Jesus in, (Matthew 17:9), "And as they came down from the mountain, Jesus charged them, saying, Tell the vision to no man, until the Son of man be risen again from the dead."

Then there was another time in scripture, when more than one person saw the vision at the same time. It was when the women went to the grave site of Jesus, (Luke 24:22-23), "Yea, and certain women also of our company made us astonished, which were early at the sepulcher; And when they found not his body, they came, saying, that they had also seen a vision of angels, which said that he was alive."

Some visions have been so powerful and dramatic that even the prophets could hardly stand it and there were times that they were even fearful, as it was with Daniel and Job. (Daniel 8:26-27), "And the vision of the evening and the morning which was told is true: wherefore shut thou up the vision; for it shall be for many days. And I Daniel fainted, and was sick certain days; afterward I rose up, and did the king's business; and I was astonished at the vision, but none understood it." (Job 7:13-14),

"When I say, my bed shall comfort me, my couch shall ease my complaint; Then thou scarest me with dreams, and terrifiest me through visions:"

Also, there are some visions that are as though one falls into a trance or deep sleep. That is exactly what took place with Peter, on the rooftop, (Acts 11:5), "I was in the city of Joppa praying: and in a trance I saw a vision, A certain vessel descend, as it had been a great sheet, let down from heaven by four corners; and it came even to me:" (Acts 10:17-19), relates that Peter didn't even know what the vision meant at first, until the Spirit revealed it to him.

Paul also had this similar experience in, (Acts 22:17-18), "And it came to pass, that, when I was come again to Jerusalem, even while I prayed in the temple, I was in a trance; And saw him saying unto me, Make haste, and get thee quickly out of Jerusalem: for they will not receive thy testimony concerning me." In this vision Paul even argued with the Lord in the vision, (Acts 22:19-20).

After my oldest daughter was born, I went back into the evangelistic ministry when she was three months old. Sometime later when she was around two to three years of age, I had a trance-like vision. Everyday I would lie down with my daughter at her naptime, until she fell asleep. She usually fell asleep in about fifteen minutes, and then, I would get up and prepare for the night service, with prayer and Bible study. But, that day in Florida would prove to be a very different day.

It was at a time in my life, that I was questioning what I had always believed to be the truth concerning some things that I had read in God's Word. But, there had been much troubling in my spirit from some of the churches where I had been ministering. For they were involved in a doctrine that was new to me and I was being bombarded with this new teaching at some of their churches. I was debating with them at every level, but I was beginning to wear down. The ministers in those churches were so strong and persuasive in their point of view that I was questioning myself, that maybe I had been wrong. That doctrine had such a stronghold, in those churches, that they were using every occasion to show me what they perceived to be the truth. At first I laughed and even made fun of them to their faces, then I debated with them. But after seemingly hearing it everywhere and even from ministers I had long respected, I was slowly becoming confused over this new doctrine of lies. I finally pulled my car over to the side of the road one day, and declared to the Lord, that if this doctrine were true, I would still serve Him because He had been so good to me. But I definitely would not want to give up having somewhat of a normal life with my family, by continuing in the evangelistic ministry for the rest of my life. Especially if there was *not* going to be a reckoning day, when the laborers receive their rewards for what they have done in the body.

Well, it was during that time, when I was questioning the Lord and myself over these supposedly new truths that God spoke to me in a trance-like vision. I had laid down with my daughter for her naptime as always. It could not have been more than five minutes into the nap when the vision began. In the vision I was laying on a couch, unconscious and dying. I could hear those around me but they could not hear me. I was trying to make them understand that I was still alive and for them not to give me up for death. I found out later that the hearing is one of the last things to go when someone is dying. The next part of the vision was of me being led by a loved-one to what looked like the top of an escalator. The person leading me to the escalator was at the same time commenting on how he would love to get on that escalator if he was in my position.

To this day I am not in agreement with the medical concept that being brain dead means the person is dead, because of what I saw and experienced in that vision. For, as soon as they let go of me at the top of the escalator, I began a downward descent into a thick black darkness that could be felt. It was as though I was on an escalator that was descending at a very high speed - like the cables had broken and the escalator was out of control.

Many years later while I was in Russia, I experienced that kind of situation on an escalator there. We were traveling down on an escalator from about the third or fourth floor at night and it was terrifying to me. For it was descending faster than any escalator I have ever been on, but it was nothing like what I had experienced in that vision many years before.

While I was still in the midst of the vision, the escalator finally came to a stop, with me being thrown abruptly into outer darkness. Darkness, like it is in outer space when the shuttle lifts off into outer space. I was being tossed weightlessly, over and over and over again in that gross darkness. I remember how weary I felt while thinking, "Will this ever come to a stop or some kind of an end?" When I finally did come to a stop, I was facing upward, where I saw above me what looked like a round earth and I breathed a breath of relief thinking it was over. When all of a sudden I flipped over and I was facing downward. That is when I saw what looked like a round ball of fire, somewhat like the sun in the sky. I said within myself again, "It had never entered my mind, I could be lost." Then the vision was over and I was shaking like a leaf, as though it had really happened to me.

    I first got my Bible out and began to read about what the outer darkness was and for whom it was reserved. I wanted to know the difference between the hell that was created for the devil and his angels, where also the unbelievers will go, and this outer darkness, that I had experienced in the vision. I first read in, (Matthew 25:30), "And cast ye the unprofitable servant into outer darkness: there shall be weeping and gnashing of teeth." That sounded to me like those who had known what the will of God was for their life, but in their rebellion they became unprofitable for God. It also was the pattern of the servant that hid his talent in the earth. (Matthew 25:25-26).

    I later realized that the outer darkness that I saw in the vision is reserved for those persons, who professed Christianity, though they teach heresy in the name of Jesus. Yet, because they choose to be called Christians, while following such abominable practices as lasciviousness or pampered indulgence of lust of the flesh. These wandering stars have caused the way of truth to be blasphemed, as in (Jude 1:11-13), "Woe unto them! For they have gone in the way of Cain, and ran greedily after the error of Balaam for reward, and perished in the gainsaying of Core. These are spots in your feasts of charity, when they feast with you, feeding themselves without fear: clouds they are without water, carried about of winds; trees whose fruit withered, without fruit, twice dead, plucked up by the roots; Raging waves of the sea, foaming out their own shame; wandering stars, to whom is reserved the blackness of darkness for ever." According to Jude these were those that once walked the right way, but for various reasons chose another lifestyle.

    Some leaders like Balaam, for the sake of gaining financially, have distorted and corrupted the

Word of God by refining away its true meaning. They, by hiding the truth of the Word of God, preach the lies of the corrupted Word for their own gain.

Core is one who becomes seditious and an ambitious head. For Core had been given a higher leadership than most of Israel, yet in rebellion to authority, he would not give honor or respect to the Lord's chosen leaders over him. There is a vast difference between being ambitious at any cost than having the zeal of God for His people and His work. Some leaders are so ambitious in their desire for leadership and praises of men, that they stop at nothing to achieve their own goal positions.

But then there are those leaders like Cain, having their false and profaned doctrines that actually corrupted and destroyed the souls of the people. God was showing me, that this so called "new revelation" was false and that it had corrupted many souls. Also I was being warned not to take my ministry into those churches, since new-baby Christians would end up in those Churches with false teachers if they saw *me* there, and because they trusted me. The Lord takes care of His little ones and will go to great lengths to protect them.

I decided on that very day, after having that

vision, that no matter what others believed, it was not going to affect my faithfulness to the Lord or what He had made known to me through His Word. I also decided that day, like King David of old, I would change my confession to, (Psalms 40:8-9), "I delight to do thy will, O my God: yea, thy law is within my heart. I have preached righteousness in the great congregation: lo, I have not refrained my lips, O LORD, thou knowest." What took place on that day to me was a vision similar to the trance Peter experienced. It was a vision that I can still see even after nearly thirty years. That vision was given to me to set my persuasion and doctrine in order, just like the vision that the Lord gave Peter to open his eyes to the plan of God's salvation to the Gentiles.

There are times that God reveals His secrets in the night vision according to (Daniel 2:19), "Then was the secret revealed unto Daniel in a night vision. Then Daniel blessed the God of heaven." King Nebuchadezzar had a vision of secrets in the night also. (Daniel 2:28), "But there is a God in heaven that revealeth secrets, and maketh known to the king Nebuchadnezzar what shall be in the latter days. Thy dreams, and the visions of thy head upon thy bed, are these;"

Some visions are not just for the one who had the vision. There are times that God wanted the vision to be told to others. Therefore He would tell them to write the vision down, like Daniel, Nebuchadezzar, Habakkuk and John, the Revelator. (Habakkuk 2:2-3), "And the LORD answered me, and said, Write the vision, and make it plain upon tables, that he may run that readeth it. For the vision is yet for an appointed time, but at the end it shall speak, and not lie: though it tarry, wait for it; because it will surely come, it will not tarry."

God still gives visions to the prophetic ministry. Sometimes they are visions in the night and at other times they are visions while the person is wide-awake. Throughout the generations there have been books written, lives changed, and people encouraged, because someone heard God's voice in a vision. *Visions are still for today.* It may be that a person has one vision, in his lifetime. Then there are others that have had many, but none are to be taken lightly, for the vision is God's voice to mankind.

Chapter 5
He Speaks To Us In Dreams

"God will make His will and Himself known to His children, in many ways, because of His great love for them."

Another way God has and still does speak, to His people is in dreams. God will make His will and Himself known to His children, in many ways, because of His great love for them. God, Himself, told Aaron and Miriam that He spoke to His prophets, through visions and dreams, (Numbers 12:6), "And he said, Hear now my words: If there be a prophet among you, I the LORD will make myself known unto him in a vision, and will speak unto him in a dream."

God not only talks to His prophets in dreams, but at times He has revealed Himself and His will, to His children, and even to some non-believers. There has been many times, that people have received warnings, from God through dreams. As when God warned Abimelech in a dream, not to touch Abraham's wife, Sarah in, (Genesis 20:3), "But God came to Abimelech in a dream by night, and said to him, Behold, thou art but a dead man, for the woman which thou hast taken; for she is a man's wife." God also warned King Pharaoh and King Nebuchadnezzar of impending trouble, through a dream. (Genesis 41:25, 30), "And Joseph said unto Pharaoh, The dream of Pharaoh is one: God hath showed Pharaoh what he is about to do. And there shall arise after them seven years of famine; and all the plenty shall be forgotten in the land of Egypt; and the famine shall consume the land;" (Daniel 2:3), "And the king said unto them, I have dreamed a dream, and my spirit was troubled to know the dream."

In the New Testament, God warns Joseph, Mary's husband, four times in a dream, concerning Mary and the baby Jesus. (Matthew 1:20), "But while he thought on these things, behold, the angel of the Lord appeared unto him in a dream, saying, Joseph, thou son of David, fear not to take unto thee Mary thy wife: for that which is conceived in her is of the Holy Ghost." (Matthew 2:13), "And when they were departed, behold, the angel of the Lord appeared to Joseph in a dream, saying, Arise, and take the young child and his mother, and flee into Egypt, and be thou there until I bring thee word: for Herod will seek the young child to destroy him." (Matthew 2:19-20), "But when Herod was dead, behold, an angel of the Lord appeared in a dream to Joseph in Egypt, Saying, Arise, and take the young child and his mother, and go into the land of Israel: for they are dead which sought the young child's life."

God also warned the wise men that brought gifts to the baby Jesus, around the same time, about King Herod in a dream. (Matthew 2:12), "And being warned of God in a dream that they should not return to Herod, they departed into their own country another way."

Because Joseph and the wise men heeded the dreams God had given them, there was protection and safety for the baby Jesus. The baby Jesus was spared from all the awful slaughtering that King Herod practiced in his reign. King Herod had ordered all the male sons that were two years old and under to be killed because of his fear of another king taking his place. Then, at another time and another king's reign, the baby Jesus was protected again, through a dream, which was given to Joseph, for the safety of the baby Jesus. (Matthew 2:22), "But when he heard that Archelaus did reign in Judaea in the room of his father Herod, he was afraid to go thither: notwithstanding, being warned of God in a dream, he turned aside into the parts of Galilee:"

Joseph and the wise men were not the only ones having dreams of warnings concerning Jesus. Pilate's wife also had a dream concerning Jesus, at His impending crucifixion. (Matthew 27:19), " When he was set down on the judgment seat, his wife sent unto him, saying, Have thou nothing to do with that just man: for I have suffered many things this day in a dream because of him." Therefore, through the scriptures, it is proven that God can and will talk to mankind through *dreams*.

God also gives *dreams of wisdom and instruction* for receiving His blessings. Jacob had numerous dreams that gave him the wisdom and instructions on how to outwit his in-laws that were trying to steal the blessings from him, (Genesis 31:11), "And the angel of God spake unto me in a dream, saying, Jacob: And I said, Here am I." That was God in that dream talking to Jacob. God had given himself a voice to Jacob, in a dream as He revealed Himself to him. (Genesis 31:13), "I am the God of Bethel, where thou anointedst the pillar, and where thou vowedst a vow unto me: now arise, get thee out from this land, and return unto the land of thy kindred."

God was giving Jacob instructions in a dream on how and where to go, so that he could overcome his enemies. God had no intentions of allowing those heathens to steal the very promises from Jacob that God had given him. God was also showing Jacob His Word, and that He would watch over His Word to bring it to pass. (Psalms 147:19), "He showeth his word unto Jacob." The God that we serve remains faithful at all times. In my own life God has warned and spared me many problems and heartaches, through dreams.

Joseph, Jacob's son, had two dreams foretelling him of his future calling in, (Genesis 37:6-7), "And he said unto them, Hear, I pray you, this dream which I have dreamed: For, behold, we were binding sheaves in the field, and, lo, my sheaf arose, and also stood upright; and, behold, your sheaves stood round about, and made obeisance to my sheaf." Then in, (Genesis 37:9), "And he dreamed yet another dream, and told it his brethren, and said, Behold, I have dreamed a dream more; and, behold, the sun and the moon and the eleven stars made obeisance to me."

Joseph would definitely need those two promises he had received from God in a dream, in the hard years ahead of him. Joseph must have encouraged himself many times, by remembering those dreams, while he was a servant in Egypt and even in prison unjustly.

Another time while Joseph was in prison in Egypt, the chief butler and baker had a dream that predicted their future outcome. The chief butler had a dream, which meant, that he would be restored to his job. While the baker's dream was of his doom and death. Joseph interpreted their dreams, before the outcome of the dreams were finalized.

God asked King Solomon in a dream what he would like God to give him, (1 King 3:5), "In Gibeon the LORD appeared to Solomon in a dream by night: and God said, Ask what I shall give thee." Solomon answered God in the same dream, (1 King 3:9), "Give therefore thy servant an understanding heart to judge thy people, that I may discern between good and bad: for who is able to judge this thy so great a people?"

After being in the evangelistic ministry for only a few years, a situation happened that was meant to cause me to relinquish the ministry in which God had been blessing me. After much consultation, I had half-heartedly agreed to relinquish the evangelistic ministry by the end of the year. But, I still wanted to finish the meetings I had already scheduled. But, before the end of the year, I had an unusual dream.

I dreamed that there was a stairway, leading upward toward heaven, where there was a four-sided transparent place or room. In the dream, it seemed to be the place where I had to go, in order to plead my reasons for the change of a garment. The garment in this dream stood for my ministry, that the Lord had given me. I went up the stairs with the garment of my choice in hand. It was the garment, which my loved one and I had agreed on. All I had to do was pay for it. So I put the money for the exchange into the new garment and went up the stairs. The garment in the dream was the covering up, of what I was actually called to do. The money was to somehow finalize the deal that I was trying to make with God. There is always a price to be paid for not doing what the Lord has given you to do.

I was taken to a room where the change of garments was supposed to take place. While I waited, I began to look into a full-length mirror at myself. As I looked at my self in the mirror, I began to admire how well I looked without the cover-up garment. Then I heard a voice say unto me, "Do you like what you see?" I answered back, "Yes, but it is too late, I have already agreed to another garment and I have come here to purchase it." I then turned around to pick up the garment, to show it to the one who was talking to me. For I wanted to prove that I came prepared to pay for the exchange. But, to my amazement, the garment was gone, with the payment in it.

While I had been distracted, with admiring how well I looked in the mirror, someone had come in and picked up the garment. I hadn't even noticed when the garment was taken, nor had I noticed who took it. I immediately started out of the room, thinking, "How will I explain to the other person what I have done?"

That night in that dream the Lord and I had come into an agreement, without anyone else being a part of the assessment, for what was best for my life. I had not really wanted to give up the ministry I had been given; I had just been persuaded that it was for the best. By the end of that year instead of leaving the evangelist ministry, I had a full schedule in churches, for the next two years. And I have remained in that evangelistic ministry for over thirty-four years. I have had the privilege and the honor, of preaching the good news in over fifty countries and have been blessed beyond my wildest dreams.

In the book of Job it is revealed why God sometimes chooses to speak to man in a dream. (Job 33:12-16), "Behold, in this thou art not just: I will answer thee, that God is greater than man. Why dost thou strive against him? For he giveth not account of any of his matters, for God speaketh once, yea twice, yet man perceiveth it not. In a dream, in a vision of the night, when deep sleep falleth upon men, in slumberings upon the bed; Then he openeth the ears of men, and sealeth their instruction," because in so many instances, God's people are striving with God unknowingly, that God chooses to speak clearly to them in a dream, of His plans or warnings.

Therefore God, out of His mercy, seals their instructions to them in a dream.

Also it is worthy to note, that when someone has the same dream, at least twice, it's meaning is that it has been established by God and it will happen shortly. (Genesis 41:32), "And for that the dream was doubled unto Pharaoh twice; it is because the thing is established by God, and God will shortly bring it to pass."

There is only *one negative side* of God speaking to mankind in dreams. It is because many of God's own people can't seem to discern, the difference between a dream that is *from God* and a dream that is of their *own* heart. That is why it is so important to know what the Bible says - so that every dream one might have can be judged in the light of the written Word of God. Remember that the Spirit of God always bears witness to the Word of God and the Spirit speaks nothing of himself. Many people have dreams that will never come to pass, because the dream is not the voice of God talking to them. But, instead the dream or the dreams that they are having is just their own longings and their own lustful desires being manifested in their dreams. (Isaiah 29:8), "It shall even be as when an hungry man dreameth, and, behold, he eateth; but he awaketh, and his soul is empty: or as when a thirsty man dreameth, and, behold, he drinketh; but he awaketh, and, behold, he is faint, and his soul hath appetite:"

In other words though they are dreaming in the night, it is only a daydream or a wishful dream. It can also be just a tormenting dream of fear that a person might have. Nevertheless, even with this one negative side of having dreams, God still can and does talk to his people in dreams.

Since I was a young child I have experienced hearing from God in dreams many times in my life. Some of the dreams I have had were warnings, not only for myself but for my loved ones, too. Sometimes, I've had dreams that spoke directly to me, as an instruction that would help me in the ministry, or with a certain situation, in my life. Other times I have experienced a dream from the Lord that helped me make a fruitful decision. But, the dreams that have meant the most to me were the dreams that spoke to me, concerning some heartache that was ahead of me. If I had not seen the end of the situation in a dream, before it ever happened, it might have been more than I was able to bear. But because of His presence going before me and leading me through the valley, of the shadow of death, I could overcome the hopelessness.

He that is always faithful will not leave you comfortless. God will make His will and Himself known, in many ways, because of His great love for His people.

Chapter 6
Discerning the Spirit Speaking To Us

"Since the time of creation, the Spirit of God has come upon man and thus becomes a voice for God."

    Today with so many voices in the world, one must know the voice of God or be deceived. And with so many kinds of voices competing for our attention, there are also just that many kinds of spirits that are making they're voice known also. But the main spirits discussed in this chapter are the spirit of man, the Spirit of God that came upon man, and the indwelling of the Holy Ghost. Though there is only one Spirit of God, which is the third person of the Trinity, there is vast difference in the ways in which the Spirit functions.

    First of all, mankind has a spirit and his spirit has a voice. His voice is *feelings*. He feels this or he feels that. Because man's voice is feelings, it is not only very loud and persuasive to the man, but it is ruled at times by the five physical senses, of touch, hearing, seeing, smelling and taste. For the most part, the spirit of the man has control of the unregenerate man. But, the born-again believer can and should be able to hear the voice of the spirit of God, thus allowing the Holy Ghost to have preeminence in their life. As in, (Romans 8:14), "For as many as are led by the Spirit of God, they are the sons of God."

We know that man has his own spirit, because God formed man's spirit, and that spirit is *eternal*, as it is written in, (Zechariah 12:1), "The burden of the word of the LORD for Israel, saith the LORD, which stretcheth forth the heavens, and layeth the foundation of the earth, and formeth the spirit of man within him." God took a measure of His own Spirit and formed man - a spirit, in, (Genesis 2:7), "And the LORD God formed man of the dust of the ground, and breathed into his nostrils the breath of life; and man became a living soul." Only life can give life! Also that spirit will go back to God, when the man dies, (Ecclesiastes 12:7), "Then shall the dust return to the earth as it was: and the spirit shall return unto God who gave it."

(Ecclesiastes 3:21), "Who knoweth the spirit of man that goeth upward, and the spirit of the beast that goeth downward to the earth?" Apostle Paul says in, (1Corinthians 2:11), "For what man knoweth the things of a man, save the spirit of man which is in him? Even so the things of God knoweth no man, but the Spirit of God." That is the very reason that man must have the Spirit of God within him as well as his own spirit, in order to know the things of God.

Then in, (Proverbs 20:27), "The spirit of man is the candle of the LORD, searching all the inward parts of the inward parts of the belly." John Wesley explained the candle of the Lord is the spirit of man that God formed inside the man. (John Wesley Notes states), "The candle-is a clear and glorious light set up in man for his information and direction. Of the Lord-so called because it comes from God in a more immediate manner than the body, and because it is in God's stead, to observe and judge all our actions."[1] Thus the spirit of man that is eternal has been put into every child that is born, for their information and direction; as well as a part of the eternal God who is a Spirit. For according to John Wesley, the spirit of man is like having God's eyes, living inside of every person as a candle. In this way

God can and does read all of our thoughts and motives. It is somewhat like all of mankind having a computer inside of him, while being connected to the main computer, which is God.

Then by the scriptures, it is settled that every human being has their own spirit that comes from God and goes back to God, where it came from when one dies. Also, until Jesus came and paid the ultimate price for mankind, man was held responsible for the actions that were committed under inspiration of his own spirit. (Proverb 25:28), "He that hath no rule over his own spirit is like a city that is broken down, and without walls." (Proverbs 16:32),"He that is slow to anger is better than the mighty; and he that ruleth his spirit than he that taketh a city."

In the Old Testament, the Spirit of God in a greater measure didn't talk to everyone, but only to the ones that God chose. For the most part, God's Spirit came upon His chosen ones to say or do something extraordinary. One can see how the Spirit of God came upon Othniel, Joshua's nephew, to judge and deliver Israel. (Judges 3:10),"And the spirit of the LORD came upon him, and he judged Israel, and went out to war: and the LORD delivered Chushanrishathaim, king of Mesopotamia into his hand; and his hand prevailed against Chushanrishathaim." God also put His Spirit upon Gideon and Jephthah to win wars, for God. (Judges 6:34), "But the spirit of the LORD came upon Gideon, and he blew a trumpet; and Abiezer was gathered after him."

(Judges 11:29), "Then the spirit of the LORD came upon Jephthah, and he passed over Gilead, and Manasseh, and passed over Mizpeh of Gilead, and from Mizpeh of Gilead he passed over unto the children of Ammon." When the Spirit of God came upon Jephthah, he would make a vow that was very difficult and would keep it, though it was difficult. . One may think Jephthah's vow was an irrational vow, but the Bible does not even give a hint that it was an irrational vow. Instead, his vow gave him the tremendous victory through God in conquering the Ammonites. Since God answered Jephthah's petition with victory, it verifies that sacrificing Jephthah daughter's life was not as the heathens would sacrifice a human life. Since Jephthah was well acquainted with the Law of Moses, which forbade such practice. He would not have even considered sacrificing a human life as a burnt offering. (Adams Clark Commentary states,) "It appears evident that

Jephthah's daughter was not SACRIFICED to God, but consecrated to him in a state of perpetual virginity; for the text says, "she knew no man," for this was a statute in Israel, that persons thus dedicated or consecrated to God, should live in a state of unchangeable celibacy. Thus this celebrated place is, without violence to any part of the text, or to any proper rule of construction, cleared of all difficulty, and caused to speak a language consistent with itself, and with the nature of God."[2]

Also, Jephthah if so desired, could have redeemed his daughter and probably that would have meant her actual death. According to (Adams Clark's Commentary), "When a man shall make a singular vow, the persons shall be for the Lord at thy estimation: the male from twenty years old even unto sixty, shall be fifty shekels of silver; and if it be a female, then thy estimation shall be thirty shekels; and from five years old unto twenty years, the male twenty shekels, and for the female ten. This also is an argument that the daughter of Jephthah was not sacrificed; as the father had it in his power, at a very moderate price, to have redeemed her: and surely the blood of his daughter must have been of more value in his sight than thirty shekels of silver."[3] Then with the understanding of what Jephthah's vow entailed, one can see why the power of God's Spirit came so powerfully upon Jephthah for victory. When the Spirit came upon Jephthah the victory was secure and he was promoted to his rightful place.

Then there was Samson, with whom the Spirit of the Lord came upon many times in his life, as in (Judges 14:6), "And the spirit of the LORD came mightily upon him, and he rent him as he would have rent a kid, and he had nothing in his hand: but he told not his father or his mother what he had done." (Judges 14:19), "And the spirit of the LORD came upon him, and he went down to Ashkelon, and slew thirty men of them, and took their spoil, and gave change of garments unto them which expounded the riddle. And his anger was kindled, and he went up to his father's house." (Judges 15:14), "And when he came unto Lehi, the Philistines shouted against him: and the spirit of the LORD came mightily upon him, and the cords that were upon his arms became as flax that was burnt with fire, and his bands loosed from off his hands."

Yet, Samson's greatest victory was in his death, when in answer to his prayer, the Spirit of God would come upon him for one last time. Three thousand mocking spectators in the theater stands would perish, as Samson holding on to the two main pillars, bowed to his God in honor and submission. This is truly "not by might, not by power but by my Spirit, saith the Lord!" Never before or since has one man ever experienced that much of the Spirit of God coming upon him, making Samson the strongest man that ever lived.

King David knew the power of God's Spirit that had come upon him, when he was only seventeen years old, when Samuel anointed Him to be the King of Israel. And the anointing of the Holy Spirit rested upon him for the rest of his life. (1Samuel 16:13), "Then Samuel took the horn of oil, and anointed him in the midst of his brethren: and the spirit of the LORD came upon David from that day forward. So Samuel rose up, and went to Ramah." Also David knew the value of the Spirit of God in his life and guarded that anointing as we can see in, (Psalm 51:11-12), "Cast me not away from thy presence; and take not thy holy spirit from me. Restore unto me the joy of thy salvation; and uphold me with thy free spirit."

Therefore as one can clearly see, when the Spirit of God would come upon someone in the Old

Testament, they would be turned into a powerful vehicle for God's voice and His voice in action.

Even from the beginning of creation, God's Spirit was there in full force moving upon the face of the waters as the third part of the Trinity, (Genesis 1:2). For after the Creator God had created space, time and matter in His universe, with the Second Person of the Godhead, the Word as it is written in, (Proverbs 8:30), "Then I was by him, as one brought up with him: and I was daily his delight, rejoicing always before him;" He the Word sat on the deep as the compass in, (Proverbs 8:27), "When he prepared the heavens, I was there: when he set a compass upon the face of the depth:" (Isaiah 40:22) The Second Person of the Godhead, before He became flesh in Jesus Christ, "was sitting upon the circle of the earth and walking in the circuit of heaven." Then in, (Job 22:13-14), "And thou sayest, how doth God know? Can he judge through the dark cloud? Thick clouds are a covering to him, that he seeth not; and he walketh in the circuit of heaven." (Dr. Henry M. Morris) states, "He that walked in the circuit, is thus a striking reference to the earth's sphericity, especially referring to the shape of the ocean, the spherical form of whose surface is everywhere the standard of measurement in the vertical, that is from sea level. The fact that this compass had to be set on the face of the deep shows that the face of the deep originally had no such sphericity. It was formless, exactly as intimated in (Genesis 1:2)."[4]

But, it would be the Spirit of God, the Third Person of the Godhead, who would transform the watery, formless, dispersion, of the earth into its form and structure. While yet in the atmosphere of total darkness, the Spirit of God began to move by His waves of motions to energize the fields of gravitation that would bring all things into order, that it had been created for. In (Zechariah 4:6), "Not by might, nor by power, but by my spirit saith the LORD of hosts." Just like He the Spirit moved almost violently with vibrations of waves upon the waters to energize the fields of gravitation, so was His moving upon Elijah so that he could out run Ahab's chariot.

As He, the Prime Mover, (the Holy Spirit), in the cosmos of the transmission of energy in the form of waves, as light waves, heat waves, sound waves, is the very same Prime Mover that had ordinary men receiving extraordinary victories and mighty, powerful works of God, which would literally be impossible for a man to do. And all this was taking place before the Day of Pentecost was fully come. Then as illustrated in previous scriptures, nothing is impossible for mankind to do or become, when the Spirit of the living God, is allowed to come upon mere human flesh, as in the Old Testament.

Unlike the animals, every human being has a measure of God's Spirit within them since the day they were born, starting with Adam and Eve. It is that measure of God's Spirit that is within human flesh that causes mankind to search after their God, with questions of why they exist. But, it is how the person reacts to the direction and information that has been disposed within him that decides his future input. Whosoever will tap into or use what God has already given them will have more outpouring of His Spirit. When one responds positive to information and direction, and then continues forward, with a desire for more, there will be even more information and direction deposited within him. That information and direction will lead one to Jesus, as their Savior.

Then as a Christian grows in the fruits of the Spirit, with love, joy, peace, longsuffering, gentleness, goodness, faith, meekness, and temperance, he will grow in his desire for the things of God, such as knowledge, understanding, wisdom, and the power of His Spirit. As Jesus Himself said in (Matthew 25; 29), "For unto every one that hath shall be given, and he shall have abundance: but from him that hath not shall be taken away even that which he hath."

On the other hand if a person quenches that measure of the Spirit of information and direction that he has been given since birth, in time, he will lose all direction and information for the truth. (Genesis 6:3), "And the LORD said, my spirit shall not always strive with man, for that he also is flesh:" This is also true after one has been born again. He can quench the Spirit of information and direction at any time in his walk as a Christian and become stagnated in the things of the Spirit. A Christian can refuse to accept a truth in the Word of God, that they have heard preached, or read, or refuse the leading of God's Spirit concerning His promises or His direction and they will forfeit that blessing.

When Adam and Eve sinned in the garden, God not only drove them out of the garden, but He took his presence, the Holy Spirit, from them, leaving them with only a measure of His Spirit. And that measure is called the spirit of man. That is why scientists have said for years that the human brain has parts or portions that have never been activated, as far back in time, as we know. The reason being is that mankind was originally created in the image of God, with God-given abilities, *like* God, but without *being* God. But, when Eve, then Adam, wanted to be *equal* with God in His knowledge, to the point of being disobedient by partaking of the forbidden tree, mankind lost a lot more than the Garden of Eden.

When God created Adam and Eve, He created them full-grown, physically, spiritually and intellectually. For as early as the fourth generation, Jubal invented both the stringed and wind musical instruments. Jabal, his brother, invented the tent for a travel home, plus he developed formal systems for domesticating and commercially producing other animals, besides Abel's sheep. Their half-brother Tubal-cain invented both bronze and iron. According to (Dr. Henry Morris), "More and more modern archaeology discoveries today are verifying the high degree of technology possessed by the earliest men. Thus indirectly validating this Biblical testimony."[5] Then man in the beginning was created with the mind of God to a certain extent. Through mankind's fall, and later the flood, much more was lost than man even realized.

  Since that time only a small portion of men were allowed the power of His Spirit to come upon them in a greater measure and then only at limited times throughout the Old Testament. No one ever again had the fullness of His Spirit within them, for over four thousand years, until the Day Pentecost, except for Jesus, the Son of God and John the Baptist.

  This brings man up to the time of the indwelling of the Holy Ghost. Whether one calls Him the Holy Spirit or Holy Ghost, He is the same Third Person in the Godhead. The Holy Ghost is described as the outpouring starting in, (Joel 2:16-18). The outpouring didn't take place until Christ had completed the work of redemption. Christ was the essential channel of the Holy Ghost and the Holy Ghost stands as a continuing promise for all future generations. (Acts 2:38-39), "Then Peter said unto them, Repent, and be baptized every one of you in the name of Jesus Christ for the remission of sins, and ye shall receive the gift of the Holy Ghost. For the promise is unto you, and to your children, and to all that are afar off, even as many as the Lord our God shall call."

In (J. Rodman Williams) it is stated, "It filled all the house where they were sitting (Acts 2:2). The *filling* the house suggests the presence of God in an intensive manner throughout them and the place of assembly. Those gathered knew themselves to be surrounded by and enveloped in the presence of the Holy Spirit. What felt outwardly in fullness then became a total experience."[6] (Acts 2:1-4) reads, "And when the day of Pentecost was fully come, they were all with one accord in one place. And suddenly there came a sound from heaven as of a rushing mighty wind, and it filled the entire house where they were sitting. And there appeared unto them cloven tongues like as of fire, and it sat upon each of them. And they were all filled with the Holy Ghost, and began to speak with other tongues, as the Spirit gave them utterance."

First of all the *tongues, like as of fire* had to be the Third Person, of the Godhead, because Moses declares in, (Deuteronomy 4:21), "For the LORD thy God is a consuming *fire*," And Paul repeats this in, (Hebrews 12:29), "For our God is a consuming *fire*." (Exodus 24:17), "And the sight of the glory of the LORD was like devouring fire on the top of the mount in the eyes of the children of Israel." The fire that they witnessed on the Day of Pentecost was God in the Third Person of the Godhead. He came and distributed cloven tongues upon each one of the hundred and twenty people. The sound that came from heaven could have been thunder since God speaks as thunder. (Job 40:9), "Hast thou an arm like God? Or canst thou thunder with a voice like him?" (Psalm 77:18), "The voice of thy thunder was in the heaven: the lightning's lightened the world: the earth trembled and shook." (Revelation 14:2), "And I heard a voice from heaven, as the voice of many waters, and as the voice of a great thunder: and I heard the voice of harpers harping with their harps:" For it was the loud thundering that Israel moved away from (God's voice) in, (Exodus 20:18) and wanted only Moses to talk to them. It was that very complaint that moved God to have His Spirit speak from *within* man, so that man could no longer put his hands over his ears to avoid the voice of his Creator.

The rushing mighty wind is described in, (Adam Clark's Commentary), "The passage of a large portion of electrical fluid over that place would not only occasion the sound, or thunder, but also the rushing mighty wind; as the air would rush suddenly and strongly into the vacuum occasioned by the rarefaction of the atmosphere in that place, through the sudden passage of the electrical fluid; and the wind would follow the direction of the fire.

There is a good deal of similarity between this account and that of the appearance of God to Elijah, (1Ki 19:11, 12), where the strong wind, the earthquake, and the fire, were harbingers of the Almighty's presence, and prepared the heart of Elijah to hear the small still voice; so, this sound, and the mighty rushing wind, prepared the apostles to receive the influences and gifts of the Holy Spirit. In both cases, the sound, strong wind, and fire, although natural agents, were supernaturally employed."[7]

The Day of Pentecost was the day Isaiah prophesied about in, (Isaiah 28:11), "For with stammering lips and another tongue will he speak to this people." God, who is a Spirit, came down that day in a mixture of fire, lightning and a mighty rushing wind to impart more than a measure of His Spirit. More than Adam and Eve had, and more than Elijah and David ever felt.

The one hundred and twenty people in the

upper room were scarecely fluent in every language of the Nations. Especially since, (Acts 4:13), tells us very clearly, that Peter and John were unlearned and ignorant men. Yet it was Peter who was the spokesman on the Day of Pentecost after receiving the Holy Ghost with speaking in tongues. It has been my experience in my many travels all over the world, that never has there been more than one individual in a group of well-educated people that could speak over two languages, besides their native language. While (Acts 2:5), clearly says that those that had come to Jerusalem were people from all the nations under heaven. Also in (Acts 2:4), says they had to have the Spirit give them the utterance to be able to speak those languages. If one knew all the languages why would he have need for the Spirit to give him the utterance?

Also, note when Peter went to Cornelius' house (the Gentile), in Joppa, (Acts 10:44-46), "While Peter yet spake these words, the Holy Ghost fell on all them which heard the word. And they of the circumcision, which believed were astonished, as many as came with Peter, because that on the Gentiles also was poured out the gift of the Holy Ghost. For they heard them speak with tongues, and magnify God." In these scriptures it is clear that Peter was in the midst of preaching when the Holy Ghost fell on them and the way Peter *knew* they had received the Holy Ghost was by *hearing them speaking in tongues.*

Then, when the Judean saints turned on Peter for being with the Gentile, Cornelius, observe his defense in, (Acts 11:15-16), "And as I began to speak, the Holy Ghost fell on them, as on us at the beginning. Then remembered I the word of the Lord, how that he said, John indeed baptized with water; but ye shall be baptized with the Holy Ghost." In that scripture of Peter's defense, he is declaring that the Gentiles received the Holy Ghost, the very same way that they did in the upper room. Which means that the Holy Ghost fell on them and they spoke in tongues. The Gentiles were not speaking with a *learned* language in Cornelius' house and neither were the hundred and twenty in the upper room speaking with learned languages. They were speaking in tongues as the Holy Ghost gave them the utterance.

In (Acts 2:4), it records that they all were filled with the Holy Ghost and spoke in other tongues. That meant, that all of them in the upper room that day received the Holy Ghost at the same time. The disciples with the rest of the hundred and twenty received the Holy Ghost at the same time and on the same day and it took the utterance of the Holy Ghost to be able to speak in tongues. The disciples received the Holy Ghost with speaking in tongues at the very same time that the others did in the upper room as, (Acts 11:15), confirms.

In (John 20:22), Jesus breathed on them and said, "Receive the Holy Ghost." This was not the *baptism* of the Holy Ghost. What actually took place in that verse was, as it was in the Old Testament, the Spirit of God came *upon* ordinary men to accomplish unordinary things. Remember the Spirit of God and the Holy Ghost is the same Third Person of the Godhead. Plus, the disciples were going to need the boldness and strength of Samson and Elijah to go to the upper room in Jerusalem to tarry for the Holy Ghost. Especially since those that had killed their Lord would be right outside the door. For them to tarry on behalf of the Holy Ghost being sent to the earth would require fasting and prayer, as well as unity in the spirit of love and forgiveness. Remember how Gabriel had to have Michael, the Archangel, to come and help him in the battle of the heavens on behalf of Daniel? Then Paul says in (Ephesians 6:12), "For we wrestle not against flesh and blood, but against principalities, against powers, against the rulers of the darkness of this world, against spiritual wickedness in high places."

Notice then later in (Acts 8:14-17), "Now when the apostles which were at Jerusalem heard that Samaria had received the word of God, they sent unto them Peter and John: Who, when they were come down, prayed for them, that they might receive the Holy Ghost, For as yet he was fallen upon none of them: only they were baptized in the name of the Lord Jesus. Then laid they their hands on them, and they received the Holy Ghost." These Samaritans were already believers who had *not* received the Holy Ghost with speaking in tongues.

Also Simon wanted to buy the ability to lay his hands on the saints to receive the Holy Ghost. He wanted that power because he could see people receiving the Holy Ghost, by seeing/hearing them speak in tongues. And he was willing to pay for it!

(Dr. Fuchsia Pickett), "The candidates who are believers in Christ are the same for both the baptism into the body of Christ and the baptism of the Holy Spirit. It is the baptizer who is different. After the Holy Spirit baptizes us into the Body of Christ, it is Christ who baptizes us into the Holy Spirit. (Luke 3:16)."[8] Also, Jesus, Himself said in (John 16:7), "Nevertheless I tell you the truth; it is expedient for you that I go away: for if I go not away, the Comforter will not come unto you; but if I depart, I will send him unto you." Jesus clearly said He would be in Heaven and would be the one who *sent* the Holy Ghost, the Comforter. While In, (John 16:7), shows Jesus was still on the earth, thus He wouldn't have to *send* the Holy Ghost. For Luke said that they were filled with the Holy Ghost first, then they all spoke with tongues. That was because they needed the *indwelling of the Holy Ghost* to give them the utterance to speak in tongues.

Jesus told His disciples that they had to ask for the Holy Ghost, just like one must confess Jesus as Lord to receive Him. (Luke 11:13), "If ye then, being evil, know how to give good gifts unto your children: how much more shall your heavenly Father give the Holy Spirit to them that ask him?" The Holy Ghost is given freely to all that *ask* the Father for Him to indwell them. Some are afraid to ask for the Holy Ghost because they think He only comes for someone to speak in tongues. Speaking in tongues are only *one* manifestation, not the whole course.

(Frank Lindblade) stated, the translators have rendered the word Paraclete as comforter. The Paraclete word is a Greek word meaning advocate, one who walks beside, advice giver, governor and caretaker. Jesus was going away but He was sending them the Holy Ghost to be more than a comforter."9 He was sending the Holy Ghost to be an advocator for His children in (Romans 8:26-27), "Likewise the Spirit also helpeth our infirmities: for we know not what we should pray for as we ought: but the Spirit itself maketh intercession for us with groanings which cannot be uttered. And he that searcheth the hearts knoweth what is the mind of the Spirit, because he maketh intercession for the saints according to the will of God." The Holy Ghost is not only a voice to us from God, but He is a voice from our inward man to God on our behalf.

Also, when the Holy Ghost came to dwell within God's people, He became their guide and teacher, as a voice from within them. The Holy Ghost will reveal the Word of God to you as you study under His influence. (John 16:13-14), "Howbeit when he, the Spirit of truth, is come, he will guide you into all truth: for he shall not speak of himself; but whatsoever he shall hear, that shall he speak: and he will show you things to come. He shall glorify me: for he shall receive of mine, and shall show it unto you." Also in, (1 Timothy 4:1), "Now the Spirit speaketh expressly." This scripture clearly tells us, that the Holy Ghost is the Spirit of truth as the voice of God speaking to us within us directly or preaching through us to others. He can even show us, what God wants to tell us or show us, from within us. As He moved upon the waters in creation, He can move upon one's heart and thoughts from within.

    The Apostle Paul tells the Corinthians that without the Holy Ghost one is unable to discern all God has prepared for them, (1 Corinthians 2:9-10), "But as it is written, Eye hath not seen, nor ear heard, neither have entered into the heart of man, the things which God hath prepared for them that love him. But God hath revealed them unto us by his Spirit: for the Spirit searcheth all things, yea, the deep things of God." By the Holy Ghost within an individual, God who is a Spirit, can and will show His people marvelous things, that is far above ones own thoughts and desires; things that He has planned and kept in store for His people, that one would not expect or dream. That is the kind of God we have the privilege of serving.

The Spirit also preached through Stephen, as the voice of God in, (Acts 6:10), "And they were not able to resist the wisdom and the spirit by which he spake." That is because the Holy Ghost was doing all of the preaching that day, through Stephen. There is a big difference between the preaching of the Holy Spirit of God and the preacher. When the preacher is preaching what he has personally studied and carefully outlined, it is not the same as when the Spirit of God takes ones voice and uses it! I have preached both ways and I know when it is only the Spirit of the Lord's outline. The preacher is amazed at what is coming to his mind as he is preaching God's Word and sometimes the words that come out of the preacher's mouth actually by-pass the mind. The Holy Ghost is preaching to the preacher as well as the congregation. Then, when the Holy Ghost is finished preaching, there is not even a thought or a word left for that preacher, it is over.

Mark says even when someone is in trouble the Holy Ghost will sometimes do your talking for you. (Mark 13:11), "But whatsoever shall be given you in that hour, that speak ye: for it is not ye that speak, but the Holy Ghost." Then in, (Acts 8:29), "Then the Spirit said unto Philip, Go near, and join thyself to this chariot." This scripture shows us how the Spirit will lead you, to those who are ready to hear God's salvation plan. The story with Apostle Peter and Cornelius house gives you another example, of the Spirit's leading us in witnessing and preaching salvation for positive results. The Spirit talked to Peter, concerning the men that Cornelius had sent to bring Peter back to his house. If the Spirit hadn't spoken to Peter, he might not have gone with them, since they were not Jews. (Acts 10:19-20), "While Peter thought on the vision, the Spirit said unto him, Behold, three men seek thee. Arise therefore, and get thee down, and go with them, doubting nothing: for I have sent them." (Acts 11:12), "And the Spirit bade me go with them, nothing doubting. Moreover these six brethren accompanied me, and we entered into the man's house:" There have been times when the Spirit has bid me to call a pastor or go to a certain town to minister when I had no intention of ever going there. Yet because I listened, there were mighty results, which could not be denied.

There are also times that the Spirit of the Lord, will try to stop you from going to some places, that if you listen, you will be spared. The Apostle Paul also heard the Lord, by the Spirit forbidding him in, (Acts 16:6), "Now when they had gone throughout Phrygia and the region of Galatia, and were forbidden of the Holy Ghost to preach the word in Asia." There is not a child of God, at one time or another who has not heard the Spirit forbidding them to say or do something. It is important to hear the Spirit of God, because as Paul writes in, (Romans 8:14), "For as many as are led by the Spirit of God, they are the sons of God." Also Apostle Paul writes in, (1 Thessalonians 5:19-20), "Quench not the Spirit. Despise not prophesying."

Because the Holy Ghost lives within us, there is a direct line to the throne room, which means He can drop information and direction to us at any given moment. Even on a job or in a crowd, the voice of the Holy Ghost can minister to one of God's children, without you having to leave the room to hear Him. Though the Holy Ghost may not be loud, He is a very real voice of the Trinity. The Apostle Paul declares that the Spirit reveals the Christ and His will to those that listen to the still small voice of

Unlocking The Mysteries Of The Voice

a great big God. (Ephesians 3:5), "Which in other ages was not made known unto the sons of men, as it is now revealed unto his holy apostles and prophets by the Spirit;" The child of God will know the difference, between what *is* and what is *not* the Spirit of God, by the Word of God. The voice of the Spirit is that still small voice *within* the believer.

    Once I was in Bangkok, Thailand with some other ministers in the hotel's dining hall having breakfast, when some of the ministers became agitated with our host in that country because we were always having to wait for them to pick us up. After some time we all decided to return to our hotel rooms. I no sooner got into my room, than the Holy Ghost told me to go back down to the hotel's lobby with my Bible in hand and sit. As I sat there wondering what I was to do next, a man from one of the greatest churches, if not the greatest in that city, came running in hurriedly, while asking me, "Where are the others?" After explaining they were in their rooms, I volunteered to go and get them, but he, being in a hurry, said, "It is too late, for we will have to run now just to make it." That day I had the opportunity to preach to many, many thousands of Thailand people as the main speaker, at three different services in Bangkok. Also, because I heard the Spirit speak that day, it opened another door in Khon Kaen, Thailand for me to minister at a nation wide Ministerial Conference.

It is extremely important to hear the voice of the Holy Ghost that speaks within the believer while in the midst of so many contrary voices that are blaring. Paul writes in, (Romans 8:14), "For as many as are led by the Spirit of God, they are the sons of God." And in (1 Thessalonians 5:19), "Quench not the Spirit." For it is the Spirit of God, that will reveal the mystery of Christ. For as Jesus came and revealed the Father, the Holy Ghost will interpret the Son of God to His own.

Chapter 7
Hearing God's Voice in a Prophetic Word, or a Word of Knowledge

"Prophecy is a voice for God to speak to His people, because only His sheep know His voice."

Another great way we may hear the voice of God is in prophecy or the word of knowledge. Prophecy is a voice for God to speak to His people, because only His sheep know His voice. Prophecy is a gift of the Holy Ghost that God uses, as He speaks and ministers to someone. In, (Romans 12:6), "Having then gifts differing according to the grace that is given to us, whether prophecy, let us prophesy according to the proportion of faith;"

Notice the gift of prophecy and it's work in the body of Christ according to, (Albert Barns New Testament Commentary), "The apostle now proceeds to specify the different classes of gifts or endowments which Christians have, and to exhort them to discharge aright the duty which results from the rank or office which they held in the church. The first is prophecy. This word properly means to predict future events but it also means to declare the Divine will; to interpret the purposes of God; or to make known in any way the truth of God, which is designed to influence men. Its first meaning is to predict or foretell future events; but as those who did this were messengers of God, and as they commonly connected with such predictions, instructions, and exhortations, in regard to the sins, and dangers, and duties of men, the word came to denote any who warned, or threatened, or in any way communicated the will of God; and even those who uttered devotional sentiments or praise."[1]

    Prophecy is a knowing of something that you would not know in your own knowledge, as the Prophet Samuel did concerning Saul's calling and what he would be in the immediate future. (1 Samuel 10:6), "And the spirit of the LORD will come upon thee, and thou shalt prophesy with them, and shalt be turned into another man." It all came to pass because it was a Word from the Lord.

    Since a true Prophet has a close relationship with his Lord, the prophecy that the Prophet or

Prophetess gives *will always come to pass*, no matter how long it takes. The reason is, because true prophecy comes from the Lord, and will always have its emphasis on the message, rather than the messenger. The gift of prophecy is a voice from the Lord that is still being used today.

The prophetic voice was used in the Old Testament and the New Testament. The Lord still uses the gift of prophecy today. This has not been done away with since His Word cannot lie and it says in, (1Corinthians 13:9-10), "For we know in part, and we prophesy in part. But when that which is perfect is come, then that which is in part shall be done away." Since this scripture was written after Jesus ascension, it cannot be talking about the Lord's first coming, but about His return. Jesus has not yet returned, so *prophecy is still for the Church today*, just as the gift of tongues, healings, miracles, and of knowledge is for today. The Church will not need any of these gifts in the new heaven and the new earth. Paul is speaking about the gift of prophecy here, not preaching the Word, because Jesus is the Word and He is the same, yesterday, today, and forever.

The gift of prophecy or the word of knowledge can be a word that is given to someone personally or it can be a word that comes through the preaching of an anointed preacher. I have had the privilege of receiving prophecies personally and during the anointed preaching of the Word.

I remember once when I was trying to make a decision, as to whether I should continue a television program in Houston, Texas. I was in the midst of wrestling with what the Lord would have me to do, when one Sunday morning at The Oasis Church in Houston, while Pastor Osteen was preaching, I received a prophetic word from the word he was preaching. He was preaching, "…the heathens are coming in, the heathens are coming!" In that message God began to speak to me prophetically, while Pastor Osteen was preaching. By the prophetic word that was being preached, I knew I was to let go of the television program and continue my overseas trips throughout Asia. For God had opened to me a great door of great favor and opportunity to reach thousands of souls in Asia.

Many times when receiving a prophecy there will be a gift or a special anointing added to the person who is *receiving* the prophecy. In that way the person receiving the prophecy can accomplish, or receive what has been prophesied unto them. This is what happened to the youngest apostle, Timothy. For Paul writes in, (1Timothy 4:14), "Neglect not the gift that is in thee, which was given thee by prophecy, with the laying on of the hands of the presbytery." Timothy must have received many prophecies concerning his ministry because the Apostle Paul admonishes Timothy, that he was well able to fight the good warfare. (1Timothy 1:18), "This charge I commit unto thee, son Timothy, according to the prophecies which went before on thee, that thou by them mightest war a good warfare;" *The voice of prophecy is for, edification, exhortation and comfort for the believer.* Prophesying is more than foretelling, it is to declare the will of God under the Divine impulses of the Holy Ghost, whether it is to a crowd or to an individual.

Prophesying as one of the gifts of the Holy Ghost is demonstrated in two different ways and therefore it is two distinctively different gifts. (1) *Giving someone the Word* of the Lord, and (2) *Preaching the prophetic Word.* as one can see in, (1Corinthians 14:22), "Wherefore tongues are for a sign, not to them that believe, but to them that believe not: but prophesying serveth not for them that believe not, but for them which believe." Since prophesying is for the *believer* and not for the unbeliever, *preaching* the Word of God cannot be what prophecy is totally about.

For the sinner to receive salvation, he must *hear* the Good News of Jesus being preached to believe. For it is written in, (Romans 10:13-14), "For whosoever shall call upon the name of the Lord shall be saved. How then shall they call on him in whom they have not believed? And how shall they believe in him of whom they have not heard? And how shall they hear without a preacher?" While revelation preaching is a gift of knowledge it is not the gift of prophecy that is given by the Holy Ghost. Even though the servant of the Lord, that is preaching may also be prophesying, while he is preaching.

The Apostle Paul says very clearly, that to receive a prophecy from the Lord, one must be a believer. Prophecy is a voice for God to speak to His people, because "only His sheep know His voice." Until the sinner becomes a believer, his spirit cannot bear witness with the Spirit of God. (Romans 8:15-16), "For ye have not received the spirit of bondage again to fear; but ye have received the Spirit of adoption, whereby we cry, Abba, Father. The Spirit itself beareth witness with our spirit, that we are the children of God:"

Then the Word must be *preached* to the unbelievers for salvation, and to believers for faith and growth. The gift of prophesying is to the believers only, otherwise, the prophecy to a sinner would be like "casting your pearls before the swine." It would only be idle words to the sinner that is not seeking for a word from the Lord. But for the believer who wants a confirmation or needs to be comforted, the word of prophecy is a fresh word from the Lord.

This is illustrated in, (Acts 9:17-18), "And Ananias went his way, and entered into the house; and putting his hands on him said, Brother Saul, the Lord, even Jesus, that appeared unto thee in the way as thou camest, hath sent me, that thou mightest receive thy sight, and be filled with the Holy Ghost. And immediately there fell from his eyes as it had been scales: and he received sight forthwith, and arose, and was baptized." Paul had already given his life to Jesus in (Acts 9:5-6), "And he said, who art thou, Lord? And the Lord said, I am Jesus whom thou persecutest: it is hard for thee to kick against the pricks. And he trembling and astonished said, Lord, what wilt thou have me to do? And the Lord said unto him, Arise, and go into the city, and it shall be told thee what thou must do." Paul being a believer now was ready to hear a *prophecy of confirmation and power* for what he was to do for the rest of his life.

Since the Garden of Eden, Satan has been taking the real things of God and making a *counterfeit* out of them; such as love - that has a counterfeit called lust; zeal - the counterfeit being ambition; and desire – the counterfeit of coveting, and on and on. So it is the same with the gifts of the Holy Ghost. Prophesy and the word of knowledge also has a counterfeit with those that are not being used by the Holy Ghost, but are using the spirit of divination. Such as we see with the astrologers and false prophets of today.

Being a false prophet or prophetess is not one who misses when they tell something to a person, but it is someone who is hearing their messages from the satanic world, as Balaam did. For Balaam caused the people of God to transgress by giving them wrong messages and counseling, (Numbers 31:16), "Behold, these caused the children of Israel, through the counsel of Balaam, to commit trespass against the LORD in the matter of Peor, and there was a plague among the congregation of the LORD."

(The Geneva Bible Notes) states, "The false prophet who gave counsel how to cause the Israelites to offend their God."[2]   A true Prophet or Prophetess will not minister or counsel *against* the Word of God. The true servant of the Lord is always sent to bring God's people back to the Lord and to do His will. Never will they suggest one to sin or to offend God.

There are people who would like the gift of the word of knowledge or prophecy, but God has not given it to them. As Apostle Paul relates in, (1 Corinthians 12:29), "Are all apostles? Are all prophets? Are all teachers? Are all workers of miracles?" Not all who prophesy are prophet or prophetess. That is the reason that some prophecies do not come to pass and bring much heartache and damage to the souls of those who actually believed they were receiving a prophecy from the Lord. Since these well meaning Christians are only guessing, at what they think the Lord is saying, they will sometimes be right and other times are wrong. What they perceive to be the Lord is only in their *own* thoughts.

When God gives the prophet a word to give, it will always be right.

On the other hand the false prophet and prophetess can be very right on, but they are not receiving their message from the Spirit of the Lord. They are using divination and sorcery, which is why they are called *false* prophets. In my opinion the false prophets and prophetess have never truly been born again, they only move in the spirit of divination. Then in receiving a prophecy, one must test the prophecy to be sure that the prophecy is coming from the Holy Ghost, and not from the human spirit or an evil spirit.

There are some things one must know *before* accepting a prophecy. The prophecy that is from the Lord will never lead the child of God away from the Lord or doctrine of the Bible. If the person giving the prophecy is trying to manipulate, intimidate, or control through fear, the prophecy is not from the Holy Ghost. The Prophet or Prophetess will belong to and be submissive to the authority of the local church and will walk in love and holiness. For if the one who prophesied is in open rebellion to the ministry of the church, as Koran was to Moses, their prophecy will be distorted.

(Joel 2:28), "And it shall come to pass afterward, that I will pour out my spirit upon all flesh; and your sons and your daughters shall prophesy, your old men shall dream dreams, your young men shall see visions: And also upon the servants and upon the handmaids in those days will I pour out my spirit." Joel is saying not only will there be an outpouring of the Holy Ghost, but with the outpouring, there will not be a gender, or position in life that is not touched, by the outpouring of the Holy Ghost. Also Joel is prophesying in this verse, that one of the signs of the outpouring of the Holy Ghost will be, that women as well as men and those of low position, as well as those of higher education would be prophesying.

Paul also states all can prophesy in, (1 Corinthians 14:31), "For ye may all *prophesy* one by one, that all may learn, and all may be comforted." Therefore this means that just because one prophesies, does not necessarily mean they are a Prophet or Prophetess. Walking in the office of a Prophet or Prophetess is more than prophesying.

Prophesying is a voice for the Lord to speak to His people today, therefore despise not prophesying, (1 Thessalonians 5:20). As Proverbs says in,

Unlocking The Mysteries Of The Voice

(Proverbs 25:11), "A word fitly spoken is like apples of gold in pictures of silver."

Chapter 8
God Speaks to Us in Song—
He Has Perfect Pitch

"A new song is a song one has never heard before right from the throne of God."

The song of the Lord is a beautiful way in which God speaks to His children. (Deuteronomy 31:19,2l), "Now therefore write ye this song for you, and teach it to the children of Israel: put it in their mouths, that this song may be a witness for me against the children of Israel. And it shall come to pass, when many evils and troubles are befallen them, that this song shall testify against them as a witness; for it shall not be forgotten out of the mouths of their seed: for I know their imagination which they go about, even now, before I have brought them into the land which I sware." (Deuteronomy 31:32), "Moses therefore wrote this song the same day, and taught it to the children of Israel." Thus God gave Moses a song that God could use after Moses' death, to speak to the Israelites. (Deuteronomy 32:44), "And Moses came and spake all the words of this song in the ears of the people, he, and Hoshea the son of Nun."

Now King David not only received the song of the Lord, but he also sang to the Lord the songs of the Lord. (Psalm 42:8), "Yet the LORD will command his loving kindness in the daytime, and in the night his song shall be with me." (Psalm 28:7), "The LORD is my strength and my shield; my heart trusted in him, and I am helped: therefore my heart greatly rejoiceth; and with my song will I praise him."

One of the greatest ways to praise God is in a *new song*, right from ones heart. The Lord can also speak through the new song of the Lord, to the singer as well as to those who have the privilege of hearing the song. A new song is a song that comes to one that they have never heard before, right from the throne of God.

King David was not only known for fighting the Philistines, but as the shepherd boy who became a king while singing and playing the harp. David encouraged himself with song. (1 Samuel 30:6), "And David was greatly distressed; for the people spake of stoning him, because the soul of all the people was grieved, every man for his sons and for his daughters: but David encouraged himself in the LORD his God." David played the harp and sang unto the Lord, which encouraged him greatly. Singing the song of the Lord has the power to mend the broken hearted and bring peace to a trouble mind, as we see in the story Horatio Gates Spafford.

Horatio Gates Spafford, was a Chicago lawyer who was delayed by some business, so he sent his family on ahead to England. They were to all meet up with his dear friend, evangelist Dwight Moody, for a revival. Within twenty minutes after they sat sail the Ville Du Havre collided with the Loch Earn and sank. Mr. Spafford's wife, Anna wired him a telegram with only two words on it, "saved alone." Mr. Spafford boarded the next available ship to be near his grieving wife. It was reported that Mr. Spafford pens the song, "It Is Well, With My Soul" on the ship around the place where his four daughters died. "When peace, like a river, attendeth my way, when sorrows like sea billows roll. Whatever my lot, thou hast taught me to say, it is well, it is well with my soul." That song from the

Lord not only ministered to Mr. Spafford, but also has ministered to countless others.

King David understood the power of a prophetic song so well that he hired prophetic singers to minister in the tabernacle of the Lord, day and night. When a person needed to hear from the Lord, he could come to the house of God and there he would be ministered to. As he would hear the song of the Lord being sung by the anointed, prophetic singers, he would hear God personally speaking, as unto him, (1Chronicles 6:31-32), "And these are they whom David set over the service of song in the house of the LORD, after that the ark had rest. And they ministered before the dwelling place of the tabernacle of the congregation with singing, until Solomon had built the house of the LORD in Jerusalem: and then they waited on their office according to their order."

Jeduthun would sing to the Lord while playing a harp and, through singing prophecy, God would speak back to him and to those that were listening to Jeduthun singing prophecy. (1 Chronicles 25:3), "Of Jeduthun: the sons of Jeduthun; Gedaliah, and Zeri, and Jeshaiah, Hashabiah, and Mattithiah, six, under the hands of their father Jeduthun, who prophesied with a harp, to give thanks and to praise the LORD." Thus the Lord can and will speak to His people, through singing prophecy. King David's practice of incorporating song into worship continued right up through the days of Ezekiel.

The song of the Lord was established under the reign of Hezekiah as he restored worship to Israel in, (2 Chronicles 29:28-30), "And all the congregation worshipped, and the singers sang, and the trumpeters sounded: and all this continued until the burnt offering was finished. And when they had made an end of offering, the king and all that were present with him bowed themselves, and worshipped. Moreover Hezekiah the king and the princes commanded the Levites to sing praise unto the LORD with the words of David, and of Asaph the seer. And they sang praises with gladness, and they bowed their heads and worshipped."

John, the Revelator, said in, (Revelation 15:3), that the Lamb, which is Jesus, gives a *song* to His people to sing. Many times while the saints are praising the Lord in song, they will receive a prophetic song in their spirit and heart. If they dare to sing the song out loud, they will most likely receive more words to sing unto the Lord.

Unlocking The Mysteries Of The Voice

How sweet it is, to communicate with our Lord, through music and song. The black psalmists in the days of slavery in America sang prophetic songs that ministered to them, as well as to the others in the cotton fields. Some of those songs are still with us today. Actually, many of the black slaves were concealing their prayers to the Lord of their grievous trials that they were enduring, by singing them. God also used the voices of the slaves, in singing His promises back to them, without their owners even knowing it. Some of those prophetic songs are coming to pass even as I am writing this. We can sing our very hearts to the Lord and He will speak of His promises back to us, in a song, even in the night season. Many times in the night season, when there was not a person to encourage me, I encouraged myself, in singing to the Lord. And He has always given me a song of promise, in the midnight hour.

We see another example of the prophetic songs when Miriam sang of the great deliverance God had given in, (Exodus 15:20-21), "And Miriam the prophetess, the sister of Aaron, took a timbrel in her hand; and all the women went out after her with timbrels and with dances. And Miriam answered them, Sing ye to the LORD, for he hath triumphed gloriously; the horse and his rider hath he thrown into the sea."

(Note Psalm 33:3), "*Sing* unto him a new song; play skillfully with a loud noise." (Psalm 40:3), "And he hath put a *new song* in my mouth, even praise unto our God" (1 Corinthians 14:15), "I will *sing* with the spirit, and I will sing with the understanding also." (Revelations 5:9), "And they *sung a new song*, saying, Thou art worthy to take the book, and to open the seals thereof: for thou wast slain, and hast redeemed us to God by thy blood out of every kindred, and tongue, and people, and nation;"

Chapter 9
The Early Church Established By Heeding God's Voice

"...God's voice will be in agreement with the holy Word of God."

There are times that God speaks through the voice of, "it just *seems* good" or, "it *seems* to be the right thing to do." One must remember, that God's voice will always be in *agreement* with the Holy Word of God. Sometimes, something may seem good and it is indeed good, because it is in the mind of God. Though it may appear to be the person's own thoughts, it is a *thought* that God has put into ones heart. Then when the thought has been acted upon, the manifestations that follow the act prove that it was the leading and will of God. As in the case of the early Church: (Acts 15:25-27), "It *seemed good* unto us, being assembled with one accord, to send chosen men unto you with our beloved Barnabas and Paul, men that have hazarded their lives for the name of our Lord Jesus Christ. We have sent therefore Judas and Silas, who shall also tell you the same things by mouth."

Also, Luke said in, (Luke 1:3-4), "It *seemed good* to me also, having had perfect understanding of all things from the very first, to write unto thee in order, most excellent Theophilus. That thou mightest know the certainty of those things, wherein thou hast been instructed." It was indeed the will of God, for Luke to write the Gospel of Luke, for several reasons. First of all, Luke was the only writer that was not a Jew, but a Gentile. Luke was the only New Testament writer out of the four Gospel writers, that traced Jesus' genealogy back to Adam, the father of all mankind. Matthew traced Jesus back to Abraham, the founder and father of the Jewish nation, while Luke saw Jesus in relationship to the whole world and not just with Israel. He related Jesus, as the Messiah, who had come to the whole world, as expressed by Luke, when showing Jesus reaching out to the Samaritans as well as to the Jews in, (Luke 10:30-37) and in (Luke 17:11-19). The same message was repeated to the poor in, (Luke 4:18), (Luke 7:22), (Luke 6:20-25), and (Luke 16:19-31).

Sharon R. Rathbun

Even though the Gospel of St. Luke was written as early as between eighty and ninety years after the death and resurrection of Jesus Christ, Luke introduces many *women*, in connection to Jesus in his Gospel, more than any other writer. Women have a very special place in the Gospel of Luke, such as Anna the prophetess, (Luke 2:36-38), "And there was one Anna, a prophetess, the daughter of Phanuel, of the tribe of Aser: she was of a great age, and had lived with an husband seven years from her virginity; And she was a widow of about fourscore and four years, which departed not from the temple, but served God with fastings and prayers night and day. And she coming in that instant gave thanks likewise unto the Lord, and spake of him to all them that looked for redemption in Jerusalem." (Albert Barns New Testament Commentary) states, "When it is said that she "departed not from the temple," it is meant that she was constant and regular in all the public services at the temple, or was never absent from those services. God blesses those who wait at his temple gates."[1]

Then this in the (Spurgeon Devotional Commentary), "Having lost her husband for eighty-four years, she had devoted herself to the continual worship of God, and had, no doubt, as a prophetess, been spiritually useful to many. Women are much more honored under the gospel than under the law. It was meet that two of the first witnesses to our Lord should be an aged man and a venerable woman."[2]

Then in, (Luke 7:35-48), "And he turned to the woman, and said unto Simon, Seest thou this woman? I entered into thine house, thou gavest me no water for my feet: but she hath washed my feet with tears, and wiped them with the hairs of her head. Thou gavest me no kiss: but this woman since the time I came in hath not ceased to kiss my feet. My head with oil thou didst not anoint: but this woman hath anointed my feet with ointment. Wherefore I say unto thee, Her sins, which are many, are forgiven; for she loved much: but to who little is forgiven, the same loveth little. And he said unto her, Thy sins are forgiven."

It was an ancient custom when a superior guest, like Jesus, visited the home of an inferior host, he would not only be given oil for his head, but be given water to wash his feet and his mouth, as well as a kiss of respect. But, Simon, a Pharisee, did not give Jesus His due respect. According to, (The Peoples New Testament Commentary), "That

Augustine said, "he withheld water; she gave precious tears, "the blood of her heart, He gave no kiss to his cheek; she covered his feet with kisses. He grudged even a drop of oil; she broke the box of rare ointment for her Lord. He treated him with despite as an underling; she adored him as a prince."[3] It is Luke's book that portrays this woman, though maybe a sinner, having more compassion and insight of who Jesus was, than the supposedly righteous man.

It was also Luke's gospel that reveals that Jesus made room for a woman to sit and learn the revelation of His Word, right along with the men where Jesus was teaching. If anyone should love Jesus, it should be the women, for until Jesus came and restored the woman back to her original place in His creation; the woman was not any better treated than the cattle. Even though Paul writes in, (Galatians 3:26-29), "For ye are all the children of God by faith in Christ Jesus. For as many of you as have been baptized into Christ have put on Christ. There is neither Jew nor Greek, there is neither bond nor free, there is neither male nor female: for ye are all one in Christ Jesus. And if ye be Christ's, then are ye Abraham's seed, and heirs according to the promise."

Yet it was Luke who shows us in his gospel, how Jesus demanded Mary's rightful place in Him. (Luke 10:41:42), "And Jesus answered and said unto her, Martha, Martha, thou art careful and troubled about many things: But one thing is needful: and Mary hath chosen that good part, which shall not be taken away from her." I remember when I was young in the ministry and I would go with my brother to different conferences. When lunch was being served there was always a separation of the men's ministry from the women's ministry. Oh how I hated it, when my brother would go into a closed room, where only the men in ministry were allowed. I would have to sit with the women listening to their latest recipe or some new fashion creation, while the men were in private, discussing the revelations of God. But, Luke tells us how Jesus would not allow Martha, or anyone else for that matter, to remove Mary from her position of sitting at His feet learning right along side with the men disciples.

It's no wonder that Renan, the famous French scholar, called Luke's Gospel the most beautiful book in the world, and certainly no book gives such a picture of the universal love of God in Jesus Christ. Luke is credited with writing the Gospel of Luke and also the book of Acts. The phrase "praising God," occurs more often in the writings of Luke and Acts, than in all of the rest of the books of the New Testament put together. We can be very appreciative and thankful that Luke listened to that voice that said, *"It seems good."*

Also the voice that affirms, *"it seems good"* is exampled in, (Jeremiah 18:4), "And the vessel that he made of clay was marred in the hand of the potter: so he made it again another vessel, as seemed good to the potter to make it." How often this scripture has encouraged the fallen child of God, to know that He who created us can and will change our character of flesh into His glorious character or nature. Jesus said in, (Luke 11:25-26), that God had withheld spiritual understanding from some of the most knowledgeable teachers and given the knowledge and the understanding to the babes in the Kingdom, because the Father thought it seemed good in thy sight.

Then again in, (Acts 15:28), "For it *seemed good* to the Holy Ghost and to us, to lay upon you no greater burden than these necessary things." For it *seemed good,* is not a voice that is *against* the Bible, but rather it will always be in agreement with the Holy Word of God. *"For it seems good"* is indeed a way one can hear, the voice of God.

Chapter 10
His Voice Through Miracles

"The unmistakable voice…"

There are times that God has used *miracles* to speak directly to an individual as when He spoke to Peter in (Luke 5:3-9). Jesus told Simon Peter to "launch out into the deep, and let down his nets for the draught." Peter had not yet encountered the power of God in the person of Jesus Christ. It was through seeing that miracle that Peter turned his life over to Jesus. With just one small act of obedience in response to Jesus' command, there was a miraculous multitude of fish. Then when Peter's partners came to help him, they all ended up with their boats nearly sinking, because of the overwhelming multitude of fish. It was the *voice of that miracle* that caused Peter to see himself as a sinner, in need of the divine purity of Christ.

Then, there was Moses in (Exodus 3:2), when the angel of the Lord appeared unto him in a flame of fire out of the midst of the bush. The miracle of the bush burning with fire and yet not being consumed was a voice from God to Moses (Exodus 3:3), "And Moses said, I will now turn aside, and see this great sight, why the bush is not burnt." It was only after Moses had heard the voice of God through the miracle of the burning bush that was not consumed, that God could talk to him further with directions and power.

I had a similar miracle happen to me in 1971, in a car wreck that should have taken my life. There were two other people, beside myself that went with me on the trip, from Springfield, Missouri to Abilene, Texas, for a family member's funeral. I had felt very uneasy about taking this trip right from the start and had expressed the concern at church. A car salesman in our church overheard my conversation with some of the other church members as I was conveying my concerns with the upcoming trip. The next day he presented me with a brand new Pontiac that I could purchase, while encouraging me that I would be a lot safer in the new car, than in my old one. Buying the new car did give me some relief and eased some of the anxieties I had concerning the trip.

Sharon R. Rathbun

There was still a twinge of uneasiness within me, but nevertheless we all left that night after work.

Since I was the one with all the concerns, I decided I should do most of the driving. There was no need to trouble the others since it might prove to be nothing anyway. I drove all night long with an occasional prayer to the Lord asking for His protection, but without telling anyone about the uneasiness in my spirit. Then around seven in the morning I turned to my sister and told her I was beginning to feel drowsy and for her to help me stay awake. We sang with the radio and talked about everything and nothing. When for only a second, while we were still singing a song, I closed my eyes. She immediately called my name. I opened my eyes and turned the wheels back where they belonged, since they had already began to swerve a little to the left. I also tapped the brakes to try to slow down the vehicle some. When I tapped the brakes, they immediately became locked and without me knowing what was happening, the a frame had broke also. I no longer had control of the automobile. By then I was pressing the brakes with all my might, with the speedometer still reading over a hundred miles an hour. After calling on the Lord Jesus for help and during the struggle of alternating between the steering wheel and the brakes, I caught a quick glimpse of a rail, which we were about to sail over. It was then that I realized I was helpless in regard to what was about to take place and cried out, "Oh My God!" And not knowing what was over the rail, I thought within myself, "This is how you are going to die." I then resigned myself to the Lord and what was going to take place.

    I didn't see what took place after that, but a farmer told me later he could hear me hitting the brakes all the way from where he was and it was quite a distance from us. He also watched the car become air-born and turn over three times in mid-air, before landing at the bottom of a thirty-two foot cliff. The car then bounced back up and landed for the second time on its wheels. When we all came to, we saw the smoke and we hurriedly tried to get out of the car in case it was going to explode. B. G., who was in the back seat of the car, his head went through the floorboard, doing much damage to his neck and his back. My facial bones had been fractured and the curve of my neck had been made permanently straight.

    We climbed to the top of the cliff holding on

to each other and waited until some one would come and help us. The farmer had called for help and a policeman responded. He took us all to the hospital. I was so shaken that I never even felt any of the pain until much later. While Donna stayed with B.G. who was immediately admitted into the hospital, I was on the phone calling everybody from Missouri to Texas for prayer for B.G's life, since they had diagnosed him with a broken neck. God, within hours, gave him a miracle because the church between Missouri and Texas prayed fervently.

      Later that night while waiting for my Mother and younger brother to come and pick us up, I went for a short walk outside of the motel. I began to question the Lord in prayer, "Why were we still alive?" For the car that we were in that was only thirteen hours old, was now at a salvage yard, completely destroyed. Even the people who own the wrecker and salvage yard had very little hope of anyone surviving the wreck and came to the hospital to see if there was anyone still alive. Well, we were alive and for what reason had we been spared was indeed my question.

      The questions in my mind were not because of going over the cliff - I understood how that had happened, but why were we able to live through it? Why was I, in particular, alive? It had only been a little over a month since I had lost my only son, Anthony with pneumonia and if I had died that day it didn't seem to me of much importance. But I didn't die and I wanted to know why. I knew I had experienced a miracle and wondered why. The miracle was we climbed out of a vehicle that was so mashed together that it looked like an accordion. Although I had lost all that had ever mattered to me, God's voice loud and clear spoke to me through the miracle, that there is something for me to do. For it was in the darkest corner of my life, of what looked like a dead end street, that a miracle became the voice of God that called me into the evangelistic ministry around the world. God gave all of us a miracle that morning in March of 1971 and spared all of our lives for Himself.

When Apostle Paul was on the island of Melita after having been shipwrecked, a viper came crawling out of the fire that Paul was making. The viper fastened on Paul's hand and injected him with his venomous poison, for all the barbarians people to see. Apostle Paul should have dropped over and died, but instead he just shook the viper off and felt no harm, (Acts 28:5-6). Because of that miracle the chief man of the island, Publius, brought Paul to his place to pray for his father who was dying. When the laying on of Paul's hands healed Publius' father, many more came to Paul for the next three months, for prayer to be healed. The voice of the miracle of Paul shaking off the viper with his venomous poison caused many to believe on the Lord Jesus Christ, on the island of Melita. Because God spoke through a miracle, a Christian church was planted in the island, which became famous for its steadfastness in the truth.

    Great multitudes of people believed on Jesus because of the miracles of healing. The healings that were performed throughout Jesus ministry were the voice of God, saying, "this is my Son hear ye Him." Healings today are still taking place and many times they are used as a voice from God to show that He is still the only true God. Plus, the Lord is using these miracles to draw people to Him in these last days of revival. It is stated in, (Robertson New Testament Word Pictures), "For power came forth from him. Imperfect middle, power was coming out from him. This is the reason for the continual approach to Jesus. And healed them all. Imperfect middle again.

Was healing all, kept on healing all. The preacher today who is not a vehicle of power from Christ to men may well question why that is true. Undoubtedly, the failure to get a blessing is one reason why many people stop going to church. One may turn to Paul's tremendous words in (Philippians 4:13): "I have strength for all things in him who keeps on pouring power into me" It was at a time of surpassing dynamic spiritual energy when Jesus delivered this greatest of all sermons so far as they are reported to us. The very air was electric with spiritual power. There are such times as all preachers know."[1]

    Likewise the ministry today needs to pray that the same flow of power will be able to flow through them so that they, like the Apostle Paul, will be able bring more multitudes to Christ. As the miracle power was put into the nets of Peter to draw the multitudes of fish, so will the Lord put His power for miracles into His servants to accomplish, a multitude of lost souls believing on the Christ. For as Jesus said after feeding the five thousand people, in (John 6:12), "Gather up the fragments that nothing be lost."

    Instead of criticizing the ministries that are

allowing the Holy Ghost to flow through them for miracles, each ministry needs to ask why he is being limited to only the ability of his mouth being used to bring the lost to Christ. Apostle Paul said that he was "made all things to all men that he might by all means save some," (1 Corinthians 9:22). Is it not the time for us to decree as Apostle Paul declares in, (Galatians 2:20), "I am crucified with Christ: nevertheless I live; yet not I, but Christ lives in me: and the life which I now live in the flesh I live by the faith of the Son of God, who loved me, and gave himself for me."

The ministry needs to cry out as Apostle Peter did in the upper room when Jesus began to wash his feet. Before Peter allowed Jesus' actions, he withstood Him, as John relates in, (John 13:8-9), "Peter saith unto him, Thou shalt never wash my feet. Jesus answered him, if I wash thee not; thou hast no part with me. Then Simon Peter saith unto him, Lord, not my feet only, but also *my* hands and *my head*." Is it not time to give all our body unto Him that He might be manifested through us in every way to reach the lost? Miracles still exits today as a voice to convey that Jesus Christ is still alive as He was yesterday and forever.

Chapter 11
The Heavenly Ventriloquist—God Speaking To Us Through Another as A Word of Wisdom

"To hear the voice of God through others, you must be careful to listen with an open heart."

Another way to hear the voice of God is when the Lord speaks through *another* person. To hear the voice of God through others, you must be careful to listen with an open heart. We see this with Naomi when she was used by God to speak a word of wisdom to minister to Ruth, (Ruth 3:5-18). Because Naomi ministered to Ruth, through the Spirit of wisdom, and Ruth received her godly advice, Ruth's life would take a drastic turn that God would use to benefit Israel. Ruth would be promoted from being a mere widow woman, working in the barley fields, to being the wife of a wealthy Israeli. She also became the great, great grandmother of King David, who had much wisdom and power in the Spirit, all because *she* listened to a word of wisdom from her mother-in law, Naomi.

The person that God uses to speak a Word of Wisdom to you, *may* or *may not* know the Lord is using them to talk to you. To hear the voice of God through others, you must be careful to listen with an open heart. The word of wisdom is indeed a voice, by which God can and will speak to you. The word of wisdom comes as someone being led to give you counsel or advice that is right from the throne room. Many times the word of wisdom works *with* the gift of discernment. They personally may not even know you are the person to whom they are ministering. The person may seek you out, or you may seek them out, for the word of wisdom.

Though the word of wisdom is a gift given by the Holy Ghost, many have never humbled, themselves long enough to hear His voice in a word of wisdom. (Deuteronomy 32:28-29), "For they are a nation void of counsel, neither is there any understanding in them. O that they were wise, that they understood this, that they would consider they're latter end!" Still others are just hardheaded and stubborn; therefore they will not receive godly counseling from anyone! When a person fails to listen to the godly wisdom that the Lord is giving them, they open themselves up to what appeals to the flesh, to their own hurt and harm. (Proverbs 11:15), "Where no counsel is, the people fall: but in the multitude of counselors there is safety."

The voice of God spoken as the word of wisdom is like receiving a key that is capable of unlocking any door of opportunity. There are two main things though one must beware of in receiving the word of wisdom from someone. First of all, one should know the life of the person offering the counseling, so that one will receive *godly* wisdom. Also, make sure there is not a *hidden agenda* that comes with the counseling they are giving you. Some counseling is not the word of wisdom, but only that person's carnal advice.

(Numbers 31:16), "Behold, these caused the children of Israel, through the counsel of Balaam, to commit trespass against the LORD in the matter of Peor, and there was a plague among the congregation of the LORD." Some ministers and counselors have been known to manipulate some trusting soul for their own advantage. Instead of ministering to a person in need of wisdom, they manipulate them for their own cause.

The person giving godly wisdom or advice will be *in line* with the written Word of God. There is not a gift of the Spirit of God, which will be in disagreement with the written Word of God. I also have found that the true word of wisdom isn't going to jeopardize your life for Christ. Also, if the person giving me counseling as a word of wisdom has given me counseling before, and it turned out to be wrong, I am very slow to hearken to them again. I look to see if the counseling they gave me was a blessing or in error. I actually prefer to receive advice or counseling, from one who has a proven ministry.

In (II Chronicles 10:8), "But he forsook the counsel which the old men gave him, and took counsel with the young men that were brought up with him, that stood before him." King Rehoboam listened to the counseling of men that didn't have any more knowledge or experience than he did, and it led to his own destruction. I have found not everyone who sounds like an expert *is* indeed an expert. Through my life I have received good and bad counseling. I personally have received counseling that was supposed to have been a word of wisdom from some ministers, but the end of the matter never happened or in some cases, brought me much unhappiness. Please, do not be foolish enough to listen a second time to those who brought you failures or heartache with their ungodly counseling before.

Some of the best counseling I have received was from those who didn't even *know* they were ministering to me with the word of wisdom, nor claimed to have a spiritual gift. The Lord has spoken to me many times through others, even when they didn't know it. Once when I was expecting my son I lived in Springfield Missouri, far away from all my family. I didn't think life could get any worse for me; I was physically sick and financially broke. I would come home from work so depressed that I would go straight to bed. I personally thought God had left me for some reason. I kept trying to figure out in my mind what I had done so wrong, to be in such a difficult place.

Even the Sunday School Superintendent where we were going to church at the time came and visited us with questions about our life. He told us that he was trying to figure out, what we could have done so badly to have so many problems in our lives. I agreed with him; that if my life had been anyone else's, I too would be asking the very same question.

Then one day our neighbors from across the

street, with whom we had never had a conversation came over for a visit. They sat in our humble living room and began to tell us of some of their early years of experiences with all the heartaches they had personally faced in their lives. They continued to speak of how God had brought them through it all and of how He had proven to be faithful. They said they had been watching us for months from across the street and saw us, as they once were so many years ago. And how God had placed it in their hearts to visit us and tell us that God still loved us and had not forgotten us. When they left I felt as though warm oil had been poured over my life of sores and hurts.

We began to visit with them on a regular basis and they were God's voice to us, during the awful trying time, when we would lose our only son, Anthony. Yet, God in His mercy put His voice across the street from me to encourage me and remind me of His promises in, (Psalm 37:23-24), "The steps of a good man are ordered by the LORD: and he delighteth in his way. Though he fall, he shall not be utterly cast down: for the LORD upholdeth him with his hand."

Another time when I was pastoring, things were beginning to get rough in our little town, where the majority of the finances came from the oil boom. When the boom was over it began to have its affect on our church and our lives. As a wife and the mother of two small daughters, I was evangelizing and pastoring at the very same time. My heart, time and life were being divided. A wise pastor, in Seattle, Washington, where I was preaching a week revival, was used by the Lord to speak to me, a word of wisdom. He began to tell me that he had once pastored two churches at the same time, plus he was ministering overseas as well. He related to me just how God had to send a minister to him, who gave him a word that actually offended him at the time.

    The fellow minister told the pastor that when he totally committed himself unto the Lord, that God was going to bless and enlarge him and his ministry. At that time, the pastor thought he was already committed to the Lord, with all that he was doing for the Kingdom. It was not until much later, that he realized, what the Lord was telling him through the man of God. The Lord really wanted him to just give himself to the one church as the pastor. When he gave up everything else, but the one church, his church grew by leaps and bounds. His ministry became one of the most successful ministries in town. It was through that pastor's word of wisdom, that I made up my mind to give up the church and go full time in the evangelistic ministry, and with the favor of the Lord, I had great success and happiness, and with my family by my side.

Also, a few years ago, when I was debating with myself about furthering my education, I received a call from a pastor whom the Lord would use to encourage me to do so. He originally thought, when he called me, that the Lord was moving him to have me in to minister on the next Sunday at his church. However, I was already scheduled to be in another state to minister at that time. But we continued conversing on the phone for a little longer, which gave me opportunity to relate to him how I had been debating about whether I should further my education. He assured me that not only should I go, he believed that I would do very well, as he had done since he had just earned his own Doctoral Degree of Ministry.

Then, God gave me another confirmation with the word of knowledge and the word of wisdom when I went to enroll in college. The President of the college at that time had heard me speak somewhere, and therefore invited my husband and I out for lunch. During the conversation at lunch, he began to relate to me how he had received a 4.0 grade average while earning his graduate's degree, but when he was earning his undergraduate's degree, he was a B average student. He went on to say how God had impressed him to improve his grade average, because one day he was going to want a Doctoral Degree.

While he was relating this to me, I knew the Lord was giving me a word of knowledge through this man. The Lord was assuring me of success in not only earning my Doctoral Degree, but with His help I could also earn a 4.0 grade average. It was that word from the Lord that gave me the faith to embark on the journey of pursuing a higher education for my destiny. Praise God, I will have my Doctoral Degree in two months with only one more course to complete, with thus far a 4.0 average.

The word of wisdom and the word of knowledge is a gift of the Lord that not only will save a person from mistakes in their life, but also actually promote them miles ahead to where they were pursuing. Remember in, (Proverbs 1:5), "A wise man will hear, and will increase learning; and a man of understanding shall attain unto wise counsels:" Wise counseling is not just for the beginner and the unlearned, but also for the experienced and learned one.

Chapter 12
Hearing God's Voice of Peace

"When the decision is the right decision, there comes an answer from the Lord, of absolute peace, directly following the decision."

The voice of peace, to the inner man, will be God declaring to the child of God, "Right on, your decision is right." (Genesis 41:16), "And Joseph answered Pharaoh, saying, it is not in me: God shall give Pharaoh an answer of peace." In, (Isaiah 66:12-13), "For thus saith the LORD, Behold, I will extend peace to her like a river, and the glory of the Gentiles like a flowing stream: then shall ye suck, ye shall be borne upon her sides, and be dandled upon her knees. As one whom his mother comforteth, so will I comfort you; and ye shall be comforted in Jerusalem."

This answer is an answer of peace. It is like when a mother holds her child without a word being spoken, yet the child knows all is well, because of where he is. This happens when one has sought the Lord for direction and then makes the decision after much prayer and thought. When the decision is the right decision, there comes an answer from the Lord of absolute peace, directly following the decision. (Acts 15:32, 33), "And Judas and Silas, being prophets also themselves, exhorted the brethren with many words, and confirmed them. And after they had tarried there a space, they were let go in peace from the brethren unto the apostles."

For example, when a person is in the right place and doing the right thing, they know it strictly by the *voice of peace*. It is the overwhelming kind of peace that God speaks to His servants. That is the reason why, when the Lord is dealing with someone to make a move or to bring a change in their life; they will suffer unrest and frustrations within themselves. And especially when a person is fighting the will of God, because of not wanting to be out of their comfort zone. They will not have His peace until they have made the right decision. They will even be miserable in what they used to enjoy. But when the child of God finally obeys Him, there will come an answer from God of total peace. I read a very interesting description of what this kind of peace really is by, (Dr. Fuchsia Pickett), "This peace means the war is over in our spirits. We are not warring anymore with our conscience or with God." It is well with my soul.

Therefore, peace is the voice from God that comes as an answer of confirmation many times throughout our lives. And it will be almost immediately when the person obeys the Lord. His abiding peace will come to them, as the very voice of the Lord. It can only be God, with that marvelous voice of peace that passes all understanding, so that the saint can declare, "I know, that I know, that I know!"

The opposite of peace is a restless spirit. One of the simplest ways God can get our attention is to make us restless. We may be going about with our vocations, or home lives when suddenly, restlessness will begin to stir within our spirits. We can't always put our finger on it, we don't know why it is there; we can't identify it, we don't know exactly what is happening, but we have an uneasiness within our hearts. It is always best to stop and wait upon the Lord in prayer. I usually will ask the Lord to show me what it is that is irritating and upsetting me. He will gladly show you what is taking place, when you cannot see but you can *feel* something is not right.

Unlocking The Mysteries Of The Voice

You may recall what God did with King Ahasuerus, when He took his sleep from him in, (Esther 6:1), "On that night could not the king sleep, and he commanded to bring the book of records of the chronicles; and they were read before the king." God had taken the sleep from King Ahasuerus, so that He could talk to him concerning Mordecai. The King had signed a decree to have all the Jews killed because of the plot of Haman. The King didn't know that Queen Esther, his favorite, was a Jew. But, since the King was awake and restless, he called for the Book of Records of the Chronicles to be brought to him. By reading the records, he realized he had not rewarded Mordecai, who had saved his life. Therefore, the next day, he not only rewarded him, but the wheels were set in motion to save the Jews as well as Queen Esther, from the plot of Haman.

Chapter 13
A Critical Choice—
To Ignore or Heed The Voice

"Our lives are so much richer and more glorious when we obey His dear sweet voice."

After seeing all the wondrous ways, that God can, will and still does talk to His children, one would think, that "he that hath an ear to hear" would want to clearly hear all that He has to say. To hear with the hearing of the ear is wonderful, (Song of Solomon 1:10), "My beloved spake, and said unto me, Rise up, my love, my fair one, and come away." Historically, the vineyard or garden of the King, here first introduced us to the Kingdom. As Paul writes in, (Romans 14:17), "For the kingdom of God is not meat and drink, but righteousness, and peace, and joy in the Holy Ghost." (Song of Solomon 2:14), "O my dove, that art in the clefts of the rock, in the secret places of the stairs, let me see thy countenance, let me hear thy voice; for sweet is thy voice, and thy countenance is comely."

But we should pursue *hearing to the place of obedience.* (Proverbs 4:20-22), "My son, attend to my words; incline thine ear unto my sayings; Let them not depart from thine eyes; keep them in the midst of thine heart. For they are life unto those that find them, and health to all their flesh." What Solomon is really saying in this verse, is that hearing the Lord's voice will make a man healthy in all the areas of his life and produce a life worth living. Only when one walks in the Spirit, can he truly hear God with expectant pleasure. The Lord not only wants us to walk in the Spirit so that we can hear Him correctly, but to rejoice at His voice, just like a baby does when hearing his mother enter the room.

The Lord doesn't want us to be afraid as Adam and Eve were in the garden, (Genesis 3:8), "And they heard the voice of the LORD God walking in the garden in the cool of the day: and Adam and his wife hid themselves from the presence of the LORD God amongst the trees of the garden." Then for one to be able to hear the voice of our Lord and Savior is as sweet as honey to us, and it is especially so when one is in the heat of a battle. (Deuteronomy

4:30-31), "When thou art in tribulation, and all these things are come upon thee, even in the latter days, if thou turn to the LORD thy God, and shalt be obedient unto his voice; For the LORD thy God is a merciful God;) he will not forsake thee, neither destroy thee, nor forget the covenant of thy fathers which he sware unto them."

Not only hearing His voice is important but *obeying* His voice. (Jeremiah 7:23), "But this thing commanded I them, saying, Obey my voice, and I will be your God, and ye shall be my people: and walk ye in all the ways that I have commanded you, that it may be well unto you." Our life is so much richer and more glorious when we obey His dear sweet voice. We are the candlestick or chandelier of light here on earth that God has created for Himself. There is a pattern for our life; it is the Lord's pattern and He will use whoever or whatever He chooses to mold us into being a beautiful, beaten, golden piece of His work. Just like He did in (Numbers 8:4), "And this work of the candlestick was of beaten gold, unto the shaft thereof, unto the flowers thereof, was beaten work: according unto the pattern which the LORD had showed Moses, so he made the candlestick."

How sweet and assuring His powerful voice is and particularly when one is going through the valley of the shadow of death, and not because of sin, but because he leads you that way Himself. When God's servant can hear the voice of the Lord to the place of total obedience, he has opened himself up for greatness. As one reads through the Bible, it is very plain to see what all God can do, for and through an obedient servant. In (Exodus 4:1-4), God gave Moses the power for miracles, because he could hear Him and was willing to obey Him.

God also tells Israel that if they will obey His voice, they will escape the terrible diseases that the Egyptians experienced, (Exodus 15:26,) "And said, If thou wilt diligently hearken to the voice of the LORD thy God, and wilt do that which is right in his sight, and wilt give ear to his commandments, and keep all his statutes, I will put none of these diseases upon thee, which I have brought upon the Egyptians: for I am the LORD that healeth thee."

We, the Church, are not under the law of the Old Testament; we are now under grace. Well, that is true. We *are* in the "grace age." Yet, with all the grace and the power that the Church has been given to overcome any obstacle, we continue to lose more to diseases and troubles in our immediate families, than ever before. We need to ask ourselves, where is the problem that has hindered our overcoming status? In (Romans 8:37), "Nay, in all these things, we are more than conquerors through Him that loved us." (Isaiah 54:17), "No weapon that is formed against thee shall prosper, in every tongue that shall rise against thee in judgment thou shalt condemn. This is the heritage of the servants of the Lord, and their righteousness is of me, saith the Lord."

Because we are in the "grace age" and have more knowledge and understanding at our disposal, than any of our ancestors, we must declare what Jesus said, (Luke 12:38), "For unto whomsoever much is given, of him shall be much required: and to whom men have committed much, of him they will ask the more." For in the Old Testament man was required by law to give a *tenth* of all he had, but in the New Testament, man is required to give *all* that he has.

Also, one should take notice of, (Exodus 19:5-6), how God promises His people if they would obey His voice, they would be a "peculiar people." Peculiar there means to be a treasure or a jewel to Him. He also said they would be a "kingdom of priests and a holy nation." Now the promise of being a "kingdom of priests" is a powerful place in His kingdom, for a priest was a chief ruler or principal officer who had the power to declare someone clean or unclean. That scripture also agrees with what Jesus said to His disciples in, (John 20:22-23), "And when he had said this, he breathed on them, and saith unto them, Receive ye the Holy Ghost: Whosoever sins ye remit, they are remitted unto them; and whosoever sins ye retain, they are retained." A real Holy Ghost filled priest must be obedient to what His Lord tells him to do at all times so, that when he intercedes for someone to come to forgiveness, that person will indeed come to repentance.

(Deuteronomy 5:24), "And ye said, Behold, the LORD our God hath showed us his glory and his greatness, and we have heard his voice out of the midst of the fire:" In this verse we find that if we hear His voice and obey Him, He will show us His glory. Many of us have cried out to see His glory not knowing that all we had to do to see His glory was just to obey His voice. The word "glory" actually means the very highest honor; splendor and magnitude of His handy work will be manifested unto us if we obey His voice. When we truly obey the Lord's voice in all that He tells us to do, His promise to us will be as, (Deuteronomy 30:9), "And the LORD thy God will make thee plenteous in every work of thine hand, in the fruit of thy body, and in the fruit of thy cattle, and in the fruit of thy land, for good: for the LORD will again rejoice over thee for good, as he rejoiced over thy fathers:"

The obedient child of God has been promised a long life to enjoy all the blessings that he will receive because he has loved and obeyed his Lord, (Deuteronomy 30:20). Then in, (Deuteronomy 28:3, 6), He promises to bless us no matter where we are geographically, as He did with Joseph. The promise that God made to His children in (Deuteronomy 15:5), says we will never have to borrow but we will be the lender. It is about time that the child of God walks in such obedience, so that he can have the faith to never borrow again.

Also this in (Deuteronomy 28:12-13), "The LORD shall open unto thee his good treasure, the heaven to give the rain unto thy land in his season, and to bless all the work of thine hand: and thou shalt lend unto many nations, and thou shalt not borrow. And the LORD shall make thee the head, and not the tail; and thou shalt be above only, and thou shalt not be beneath;"

The truth is, a person doesn't know what his good treasures are that God has hidden, until they hear and obey His voice. Then, and only then, does He open His hidden treasures to us to behold. Time and time again I have seen, that it was only after I obey His voice, even when I thought it was not in my best interest, I would literally be amazed at what He, the Creator, had orchestrated for my life. Remember Peter's experience on the day that Jesus had him cast his nets on the right side of the boat? Even though Peter was tired and didn't expect any thing good to come out of his obedience, he obeyed the voice of the Lord, and the blessing overtook him: a blessing that reached his partners as well as himself. As one can see then, *it is impossible to obey the Lord if you are not acquainted with His voice.* I remember that as a child, sometimes I didn't even have to hear my earthly Dad's voice to know that he was talking to me; I could feel him and his eyes, even from distance.

I believe the more intimately the child of God becomes with his Lord and His voice, that even before He speaks, there is a feeling by His Spirit within you what the Lord is saying. Even when it is a feeling of His displeasure or His grieving over you, as He did about making man in, (Genesis 6:6), "And it repented the LORD that he had made man on the earth, and it grieved him at his heart." Or, the grieving that He felt with Israel in, (Psalm 95:10), "Forty years long was I grieved with this generation, and said, It is a people that do err in their heart, and they have not known my ways:" Or in, (Mark 3:5), "And when he had looked round about on them with anger, being grieved for the hardness of their hearts."

The servant that really loves Him and His presence has no desire to grieve Him in any way. The Apostle Paul says in, (Ephesians 4:30), "And grieve not the Holy Spirit of God, whereby ye are sealed unto the day of redemption." Just as you can sense His *displeasure*, you can also feel His *pleasure* when you have done the right thing in some matters, that perhaps only He and you know. (1 Chronicles 29:17), "I know also, my God, that thou triest the heart, and hast pleasure in uprightness." (Psalm 35:27), "Let the LORD be magnified, which hath pleasure in the prosperity of his servant."

Oh, how He loves to see His people in the right place, doing the right things according to their calling and loving Him for who He is and where He has brought them. Praise God!

For all people and all things were created *by* Him and *for* Him, (Revelation 4:11), "Thou art worthy, O Lord, to receive glory and honour and power: for thou hast created all things, and for thy pleasure they are and were created.

To know and hear His voice is a great pleasure for His children, but just as much pleasure to our Lord!

Selected Bibliography

Barclay, William. *The New Testament*: Copyright © 1968, (Westminster John Know Press, Louisville, Kentucky)

Feinberg, Charles L. *The Minor Prophets*: Copyright © 1948, (Moody Press, Chicago, Illinois)

Hitchcock, Mark, *The Complete Book Of Bible Prophecy*: Copyright © 1999, (Tydale House Publishers, Inc. Wheaton, Illinois, 60189)

Jamirson, Robert. *Jamirson-Fausset-Brown Commentary*: Copyright © 1871, (e_stefanik©email.msn.com. Bronson, Michigan, 49028)

Lindblade, Frank. *The Spirit, Which Is From God*: Copyright © 1928, (Gospel Publishing House, Springfield, Missouri):

Linder, Phil. *Adam Clark's Commentary*: Copyright © 2002, (Online Publishing, Inc., Bronson, Michigan, 49028)

Linder, Phil. *Albert Barns New Testament Commentary*: Copyright © 2002, (Online Publishing, Inc. Bronson, Michigan, 49028)

Linder, Phil. *Geneva Bible Notes*: Copyright © 2002, (Online Publishing, Inc., Bronson, Michigan, 49028)

Linder, Phil. *Matthew Henry's Commentary On The Whole Bible*: Copyright © 2002, (Online Publishing, Inc. Bronson, Michigan, 49028)

Linder, Phil. *John Wesley' Notes On The Old And New Testament*: Copyright © 2002, (Online Publishing, Inc. Bronson, Michigan, 49028)

Linder, Phil. *Power Bible*: Copyright © 2002, (Online Publishing, Inc. Bronson, Michigan, 49028

Linder, Phil. *Spurgeon Devotional Commentary*: Copyright © 2002, (Online Publishing, Inc. Bronson, Michigan, 49028)

Moo, Douglas J. *The Epistle to the Romans*: Copyright © 1976, (William B. Eerdmans Publishing Co. Grand

Morris, Henry M. *Scientific Creationism*: Copyright © 1974, (Master Books, Inc. Green Forest, AR., 72638)

Morris, Henry M. *The Genesis Record*: Copyright © 1976, (Baker Book House, Grand Rapids, Michigan, 49516)

Pickett, Fuchsia. *Presenting the Holy Spirit*: Copyright© 194, (Destiny Image Publishers. Shippensburg, PA. 17257)

Scott, John R. W. *The Message Of Acts*: Copyright © 1973, (Inter-Varsity Press, Downers Grove, Illinois, 60515)

Williams, Rodman J. *Renewal Theology*: Copyright © 1996, (Zondervan. Grand Rapids, Michigan, 49530

The Story Of Horatio Gates Spafford: Copyright © 1871, (http://www. Angelfire.com/ms/spiritual/) P 16.html

Endnotes

Chapter 2

1. Phil Linder, Geneva Bible Notes: (Bronson, Michigan. Online Publishing Inc. 2002)
2. Adam Clark, Adam Clark's Commentary: (Bronson, Michigan. Online Publishing Inc. 2002)
3. Clark,
4. Clark,
5. Jamieson-Fausset-Brown, Jamieson-Fausset-Brown Commentary: (Bronson, Michigan. Online Publishing Inc. 2002)
6. J. Rodman Williams, Renewal Theology: (Grand Rapids, Michigan. Zondervan Publishing. 1996). P.182

Chapter 3

1. J. Rodman Williams, Renewal Theology: (Grand Rapids, Michigan. Zondervan Publishing. 1996). P.182

Chapter 6.

1. Adam Clark, Adam Clark's Commentary: (Bronson, Michigan. Online Publishing Inc. 2002)
2. John Wesley, John Wesley Notes: (Bronson, Michigan. Online Publishing Inc. 1999)
3. Adam Clark,
4. Adam Clark

5. Henry M. Morris, The Genesis Report. (Grand Rapids, Michigan. Baker Books. 1976) P 51
6. Morris, P. 147
7. J. Rodman Williams, Renewal Theology: (Grand Rapids, Michigan. Zondervan Publishing. 1996). P.144
8. Adam Clark,
9. Pickett, Fuchsia, Presenting the Holy Spirit: (Shippensburg, Pa. Destiny Image Publishers. 1994). P. 3
10. Frank Lindblade, The Spirit Which Is From God: (Springfield, Missouri. Gospel Publishing House. 1928). P. 15

Chapter 7.

1. Albert Barns, Albert Barns New Testament: (Bronson, Michigan. Online Publishing Inc. 2002)
2. Phil Linder, Geneva Bible Notes: (Bronson, Michigan. Online Publishing Inc. 2002)

Chapter 9.

1. Albert Barns, Albert Barns New Testament Commentary: (Bronson, Michigan. Online Publishing Inc. 2002)
2. Spurgeon, Spurgeon's Devotional Commentary: Bronson, Michigan. Online Publishing Inc. 2002)
3. Phil Linder, The Peoples New Testament Commentary: (Bronson, Michigan. Online Publishing Inc. 2002)

Chapter 12.
1. Fuchsia Pickett, Presenting The Holy Spirit: (Shippensburg, PA. Destiny Image Publishers. 1994) P. 165

Chapter 13.
1. Phil Linder, Geneva Bible Notes: (Bronson, Michigan. Online Publishing Inc. 2002)
2. Phil Linder, (Treasury Of David: (Bronson, Michigan. Online Publishing Inc. 2002)

Contact Information

Contact Dr. Sharon R. Rathbun or
order more copies of this book at

TATE PUBLISHING, LLC

1716 West State Highway 152
Mustang, Oklahoma 73064

(888) 361 - 9473

TATE PUBLISHING, LLC

www.tatepublishing.com